Port Blakely

THE COMMUNITY CAPTAIN RENTON BUILT

ANDREW PRICE, JR.

published by
Bainbridge Island Historical Society

Port Blakely: The Community Captain Renton Built

First Edition Copyright © 1989 by Andrew Price Jr.
Second Edition Copyright © 2005
by Bainbridge Island Historical Society

For information contact
Bainbridge Island Historical Society
215 Ericksen Ave. NE
Bainbridge Island WA 98110
206-842-2773
www.bainbridgehistory.org

Library of Congress Catalog Card Number:
89-92537
ISBN: 0-9715147-1-2
Book and cover design by Virginia Hand

This book is dedicated to my mother and father
who bought a home on Restoration Point in 1929.
For most years since then, it has been a happy summer
destination for our family. It is also dedicated
to my wife, Marianna, and our children who never told me,
although they may have had reason to, that they had heard
more about Port Blakely and Captain Renton than they
really wanted to. To a great extent, my interest became their
interest and for this, as for so much in our lives together,
I shall always be grateful.

INDIVIDUALS WHOSE HELP AND
ENCOURAGEMENT WERE IMPORTANT

Freda Adams, resident of Ryderville and Toe Jam Hill and spirited friend, now departed.

Pilar Astorquiza, University of Chile, Santiago. She found records of shipments of Douglas fir from Puget Sound to the nitrate fields of Chile.

Richard C. Berner, Archivist, University of Washington, Retired. His fascination with the archival material in the Port Blakely Mill Company records was infectious.

Donna Bline, Seattle. She wrestled with one of my numerous redrafts and thereby helped the project along.

Garret Eddy, Chairman, Port Blakely Mill Company and Port Blakely Tree Farms. He gave me permission to review early company records and encouraged me through years of research and writing.

Gerald Elfendahl, Winslow. My thanks for his intelligent and persistent efforts to preserve and make known the history of Port Blakely and other Bainbridge Island communities and landmarks.

Agnes Ellefsen, president of the Port Blakely Cemetary helped me locate descendents of early families and entrusted much cemetary information to me.

Virginia Hand, Seattle. To her go my sincere thanks for designing the book and shepherding it through two printings.

Captain Harold D. Huycke, respected martitime historian, encourager and friend.

Kaoru Ichihara, Seattle First Baptist Church historian, for information about Japanese Baptist Mission at Yama.

Dan Iturri, Long Beach, California, for his family story.

Cathy Johnson, Seattle. For her grammatical and editorial review.

Jean Ward Keiler, Mill Valley, California, for helping me to better appreciate the accomplishments of her grandfather, George E. Billings.

Mrs. Silas Sumner Kellam, daughter-in-law of Dr. C. C. Kellam for her gifts of pictures and memorabilia of Dr. Kellam.

Stuart C. and Mary Kierulff, Piedmont, California; grandson of Charles S. Holmes and contributor of family information and earliest photographs of new 1888 Port Blakely mill.

Ralph Kono, son of Hanjiro and Fuji Kono, who tramped the underbrush of Yama with me and made buildings and homes appear before us.

Sverre and Elsie Lund, life-long resident of New Sweden, for sharing their knowledge of that era.

Esther Elofson Lund, granddaughter of Nils and Fausta Elofson, friend from the day I met her at the inception of the research for this story.

Ernest and Veola Lundgren, long time residents of Port Blakely, in whose house I was always welcome. Both have died now. I cherish their

Theresa Morrow, Bainbridge Island, herself a writer and editor, for her
interest, research and substantial editorial contribution, which she
will recognize.

Isami Nakao, Winslow. Almost as much as I did, Sam wanted to see this
story told. He lived in Yama and through him I met others who
had lived there. I am grateful for his trust and confidence and for
his friendship and that of his wife, Kay.

Andrew Nesdall, sailing ship historian who identified previously unidentified
ships in pictures of vessesls loading at Port Blakely.

Charlie Olson, life-long resident of West Blakely with a keen memory of his
early 20th century neighbors.

Bernard B. Pelly, now departed, long-time resident on Bean's Bight Road;
lifelong family friend. He showed me the Abstract of Title to his
property, once part of the Nils Elofson property. That document
excited this project into being.

Helen Peterson, Seattle, made early New Sweden come to life.

MacMillan Pringle, Seattle, descendent of Captain Renton's sister, Mary
Renton Campbell. My lifelong friend, he made the Renton letters
and other family memorabilia available to me.

Mary Randlett, Bainbridge Island photographer of note and impatient friend
who pushed me when I needed pushing.

Vesta Rich, niece of Dr. C. C. Kellam, who acquainted me with his and her
New York birthplace.

Dee Salvino, Seattle entrepreneur in word and data processing, helped
complete the project.

Chiye Shigemura Umezuka, Los Angeles, daughter of Mr. and Mrs. Sohichi
Takahashi Shigemura, early Japanese residents of Port Blakely. Her
photographic memory of who lived where in Yama gave me a clear
sense of the reality of the place.

Katy Welfare Warner, Pleasant Beach, born on and life-long resident of
Bainbridge Island and long-time Bainbridge Island historian and
writer; ever helpful friend.

L. G. "Bud" White, teacher and historian of Pictou, Nova Scotia, who had an
immediate empathy with my interest in Captain Renton.

AUGUST 2005

I am grateful to the Bainbridge Island Historical Society for supporting the
publication of a second printing of this story, and especially grateful to our
son-in-law, Ralph Cheadle, and to fellow historian Jack Swanson for their
help to me in bringing this second printing to fruition.

Andrew Price, Jr.

TABLE OF CONTENTS

LIST OF ILLUSTRATIONS

PREFACE

T he story in your hands is about the town of Port Blakely, its founder, Captain William Renton, and about the people whose ambitions, hopes and spirit of adventure caused them to come to Port Blakely and make it their home. It is about the Captain's very successful sawmill and about the mill's neighbor, a very successful shipyard.

When one looks at quiet Blakely Harbor today, it's hard to imagine the thriving and ethnically diverse community that once was here. I hope that "Port Blakely: The Community Captain Renton Built", will make it come alive for each of you.

I have spent many interesting hours and days during the past 10 years querying people and visiting places where I thought I might learn something about Port Blakely. New friendships have resulted from the search, and there have been numerous moments of jubilation when unexpected new letters, photographs or other information suddenly came to light.

The mill town of Port Blakely, in Washington Territory, was founded in 1863. That was only 22 years after Lieutenant Charles Wilkes named Blakely Harbor and discovered that the harbor was located on an island, which he named Bainbridge. During the late 1880s, the sawmill there was said to be the largest in the world. The shipyard is remembered as having built some of Hawaii's earliest inter-island steamers and some of the most graceful and swiftest of the Pacific Coast lumber schooners.

By 1937, when ferry service to the harbor ceased, the sawmill and shipyard were long gone. Today Blakely Harbor, surrounded again by tall green firs, is home to about twenty families. On summer weekends it is a haven for yachters.

No one can predict the future with accuracy, but it seems certain that the population of Bainbridge Island, so close to Seattle, is destined to continue to grow. Some day Blakely Harbor may look quite different again. Most of us who have known its tranquility since 1937 hope that time will be far off. But whether it grows or stays the same, future generations will want to know "what used to be here".

This book is dedicated, not only to my family, but also to the memory of those who built "what used to be here", to the many wonderful men and women, in so many places, who contributed to my knowledge of the community and its citizens, and to the curious who will come later.

Andrew Price, Jr.
Restoration Point
Bainbridge Island, WA
November, 1989

CHAPTER ONE

THE EARLY YEARS—
WILLIAM RENTON EARNS HIS
CAPTAIN'S PAPERS, MARRIES,
AND LATER REACHES
SAN FRANCISCO

William Renton was born in Pictou, Nova Scotia, on November 2, 1818. Pictou was an important sawmilling and shipbuilding town on a large well-protected harbor on the south shore of Northumberland Strait. It is about half way between the border of New Brunswick and the channel that forms Cape Breton Island. Twenty miles to the north, across the Northumberland Strait, lies Prince Edward Island. Forests of spruce, pine, and fir once covered the countryside around the town. There was some farming and dairying. Coal was mined nearby.

The earliest settlers of what we call Nova Scotia, meaning New Scotland, were the French, who called this place 'Acadie'. In a struggle immortalized in Longfellow's saga "Evangeline", the British took over the land and deported the French. That was in 1755. Scots were among the first of the newcomers. Closer to the time of the American Revolution, these new settlers were joined by 'Loyalist' families, families which remained loyal to the crown of England and therefore had to flee the revolting colonies. Later still more settlers arrived in the colony from England as well as Scotland.

William Renton's father, Adam Harvey Renton, was born in 1782 in Shields, an important coal port on the northeast coast of England. The first record of his being in Nova Scotia is in the 'Port List' for Halifax for the year 1817. The list shows Adam as master of the 116-ton, 65 foot, two masted brig *Pictou,* a good sized vessel for the day and one owned by a prominent merchant of the town of Pictou. A later document, dated 1818, is an application by Adam Harvey Renton for a 200 acre land grant, preferably in the vicinity of Pictou. The document records that he served in the Royal Navy for thirteen years and that he had lived in Nova Scotia for three years immediately preceeding the date of the application, or since 1815. There is no evidence of any subsequent grant of land to him.

William's mother, Margaret Pagan Rogers Renton, was born in Pictou in 1791. Her parents, James and Mary Louisa Rogers, were members of the Scottish community in Pictou, and are believed to have been 'Loyalists' who moved there from the colony of Maryland.

Margaret and Adam were married soon after Adam arrived from England. They had five children. The eldest, I think, was a boy, James. Then came William in 1818, then three sisters, Elizabeth in 1819, Mary in 1820 and Margaret in 1823. Adam Renton died in Halifax in July, 1829, at the age of forty-seven. He is buried in Haliburton Cemetery in Pictou. William was eleven years old. Older brother James, sometimes out of touch with the family for extended periods, seems not to have been a responsible elder son, so William became the principle provider for his mother and sisters.

By the time he was eighteen, William had emigrated from Nova Scotia to the United States and become an officer on the merchant ship *Harriet Rockwell*, out of Portsmouth, New Hampshire. That was in 1836. By 1840 he had moved on to Philadelphia. Nothing was known about his next few years, except for port records in the Philadelphia Maritime Museum, until a group of sixteen letters was found that covers the period from 1840 to 1849. They establish that William was married in 1841 and that his home was in Philadelphia for the next eight years. Most of the letters were written by him or his wife to his mother in Pictou. They give as personal a glimpse into these years as one could hope to get.

August 18, 1840

Dear Mother,

I now take this opportunity to write you a few lines, hoping to find you in good health, which cleaves to me at present. Thank God for it.

I am going up the Mediterranean as Chief Mate of a new brig. I have been Second Mate of the ship *Algonquin,* Liverpool Packet, for the last 18 months. I now leave her to do better.

I am doing well and hope to continue so. I am in a fare way to have charge of a ship soon. A number of friends here that will assist me. And I must say that this is the finest Country that I have ever been in.

You need not expect me home for some time, God knows when. Do not think hard of my not leaving now. I have many thing to prevent me. When I get to be Capt. then I will return and let some of my good friends see that Renton's son will get ahead by his own merits, and no thanks to them.

Nothing more at present from your sincere & most affectionate son,

Wm. Renton

Please to send a letter as soon as possible and direct it as follows:

Joseph Sylva, No. 8, Corner of Pine St.,
Philadelphia, Penn.

William must really have meant what he wrote, when he said "this is the finest Country that I have ever been in", for less than a year later he applied for U.S. citizenship. In his application he declared before a court in Philadelphia "that he had resided within the limits and under the jurisdiction of the United States of America three years next preceding his arriving at the age of twenty one" and that "including the three years of his minority, he had resided within the limits and jurisdiction of the United States of America five years and upwards". He became a citizen of the United States at age twenty-three in August of 1841.

Joseph Sylva, to whose address Renton requested his

mother send her letters, was a successful young sea captain. Renton boarded at the Sylva home. Whether this was before or only after a tragedy at sea took Sylva's life and made Mrs. Sylva a widow is not known, but Captain Sylva's misfortune changed Renton's life, as another letter from Renton to his mother describes.

August 5, 1841

Dear Mother,

I now take my pen in hand to write you a few lines, hoping they shall find you in good health, which cleaves to me at present. Thank God for it.

I received your letter of the twenty fifth of May, and was much pleased to receive the certificate from the Rev. Mr. Elliott, making my age nearly 23 when I expected it was 24. I was married on the second of this month to Mrs. Sylva, the lady that I boarded with ever since I sailed out of this port. She is a widow and the mother of three small children. And in very good circumstances.

I expect to take charge of the brig tomorrow, bound to the island of Madeira; from there up the Mediterranean and home.

Mrs. Renton will write to you again in a short time. Give my best regards to my sisters, likewise to all inquiring friends and relatives. So no more at the present time.

Your affect. son,
William Renton

This letter of August 5th has these two additional paragraphs, the first being Sarah's first communication with her mother-in-law, the second being Renton's closing "aside" to his mother. Those two paragraphs follow:

Dear Mother,

I expect you will be a little surprised at receiving these few lines from one that you are not acquainted with, but I hope will be hereafter. I wish you to write at every opportunity, which will always be answered with pleasure. The children are too young to know the meaning of sending their love to you. So I will conclude by sending my love to you and all the family. So no more from your affectionate daughter,

Sarah M. Renton

Please to direct the letters as before to avoid mistakes. I have done better than you expected. She has one thousand dollars out at 6 per cent interest and about one thousand in cash at home.

Sarah's three children were Mary Ann, age eight, Elizabeth, age four, and Josephine Sylva, the youngest. In Renton's view, Sarah came to him with a very handsome dowry, in addition to the children. She and her new husband made their home in Philadelphia for the next eight years following their marriage. The family continued to live in the Sylva house at 8 Pine Street for a while, but later moved to 8 Catherine Street.

Less than a year after her marriage, Sarah wrote that William "has purchased one half of the brig *E. D. Wolfe*, the same one he has been master of these last two voyages". From this time on Renton was addressed and referred to as Captain Renton. Perhaps it was because in Nova Scotia "anybody who was anybody" was addressed as Captain that Renton never declined to be addressed as Captain Renton, even long after he had left the sea. As to the purchase of a half interest in the *E. D. Wolfe*, events half a century later and 'half a world' away suggest that the purchase was made from Sarah's dowry, or more precisely, from funds left to her in her first husband's estate.

Port records in Philadelphia show that Renton sailed from that city on March 30, 1842, for Genoa, Italy, as captain of the brig *E. D. Wolfe*. He had a crew of seven.

In the following years Captain Renton sold his interest in the *E. D. Wolfe* and bought part of the brig *Gardiner H. Wright*, sold his interest in her and bought all of the brig *Amanda*, and finally sold her and bought the new brig, *Mary and Jane* in the summer of 1848. He wrote his mother that "she cost about $8000," and that he "still owed about $2000 on her". He said he could payoff that debt by selling some other property, but would not do that. He was confident that if nothing happened, the debt would soon be paid off and that then he and Sarah and the girls would "come and see you".

His and Sarah's letters recount these developments and tell of trips, to the island of Madeira, the Mediterranean, Genoa, Jamaica, Trinidad and Cuba. They tell of surviving a damaging storm off New Orleans and of delivering corn to Ireland during the famine of 1846–47. Later information reveals the important influence this latter trip had on his life. Letters speak of his frustrated efforts to find his brother, of sending money home to his mother in Pictou, of his affection for her and his sisters, and of his and Sarah's hope to visit home and see them all, a hope that was never realized.

The next to last letter to survive from this period was written from New York. In it Renton wrote that Sarah and the girls were with him and that an awful epidemic of cholera had broken out. They were going to Bangor, Maine, and it is from there that the last letter of this period was written. It was dated August 11, 1849, and in it Renton told his mother of his plans. He said he was loading, likely with lumber, for Madeira, and that he didn't expect to return for six or possibly seven months. Letters could be sent to him c/o Brett & Rose, 28 South Street, New York.

In the letter is this legible but tantalizingly incomplete sentence, "We are well and loading for Madeira. A market very likely to River Plate."

The River Plate, between Argentina and Uruguay, was much, much farther south than Renton had ever sailed before. There was no mention of the thought, but could he have been planning to sail to California? Word about the gold strike there had reached Philadelphia and New York; perhaps he had already decided to go. Might he not have wanted Sarah to know what was in the back of his mind?

There are no more letters, but the voyage, as Captain Renton later related it, did take them to Madeira, where a quarantine kept his ship from discharging her cargo. He learned or speculated that there would be a market for lumber in the Cape Verde Islands, off Dakar on the west coast of Africa, and sailed for port there. Successful in selling his lumber, he took on a cargo of salt and sailed for the River Plate.

If he had been planning to go to California, and had been successful in keeping the plan secret up to this point, the secret certainly had to come out now. The record of the rest of the voyage is scanty at best. Many years later, only two months before his death, the Captain recalled his arrival in San Francisco on the *Mary and Jane* and its subsequent sale. If there was any doubt about his being an able skipper, none could remain after what must have been a near mid-winter passage from east to west through the Straits of Magellan.

The five Philadelphians arrived in San Francisco on August 15, 1850, a year and four days after Renton wrote his mother from Bangor that he would be back in six, possibly seven, months.

૨▲

CHAPTER TWO

THE CAPTAIN COMES TO PUGET SOUND, ALKI AND PORT ORCHARD

Instead of joining the rush of fortune-seekers gambling on finding gold, Renton applied his considerable energies to something far more solid: he became a dealer in lumber. There was a ready market for lumber in booming San Francisco and Renton must have been familiar with the business from his trips to Maine for lumber cargoes. For two years after he arrived in San Francisco, he is believed to have operated a retail lumber business from the beached hulk of an abandoned sailing ship.

In 1852, just before his thirty-fourth birthday, Renton made his first trip to Puget Sound. He captained the bark *Alabama* on a voyage north and up the Sound to Steilacoom in Washington Territory. He returned to San Francisco with a load of piling, leaving Steilacoom on October 26 and reaching San Francisco Bay on November 7. There he sold his cargo to the Pacific Mail Company at Benicia in Marin County north of San Francisco. He liked what he saw on the Sound and recognized that a great opportunity awaited the person who could put together the capital for a sawmill, locate and manage the mill properly and have a partner in San Francisco to market its products.

Renton was only one of the many would-be lumbermen who were scouting the territory. Among them was J. J. Felt who started a sawmill at Appletree Cove, south of present day Kingston. Blown from its exposed site there, the mill was moved to Port Madison, where it was operated for years by George A. Meigs. Captain W. C. Talbot arrived in July of 1853 and the Hood Canal area appealed to him. Finding W. B. Sayward at the site which became Port Ludlow, he chose a location across the canal at a place the Indians called Teekalet. Today we know the harbor as Port Gamble, and Talbot's sawmill operated there until December 15, 1995, having run almost continuously for more than 140 years.

In his search for a site, Renton met Charles C. Terry and discussed his idea of building a sawmill. Terry had just begun to promote the development of a village at Alki Point, in present day West Seattle, and he persuaded Renton to place his mill there. In San Francisco, Renton found backers in James Laidley and William Force and purchased equipment for a small mill, sending it along to Alki in early 1853. Writing in 1905 of his first visit at Alki in early June of 1853, pioneer Ezra Meeker recalled, "Captain William Renton had built some sort of a sawmill here, that laid the foundation to his great fortune accumulated later at Port Blakely."

Almost as soon as Renton's mill was built and in production, problems occurred. In 1888, another pioneer, A. A. Denny, wrote, "It now seems strange that men of such marked intelligence and experience as they (Captain Renton and J. J. Felt) possessed could have overlooked and passed by such superior locations as Madison and Blakely. I suppose it was on the theory that Puget Sound is all a harbor, and it was not necessary to be particular." Captain Renton learned quickly that he should have been particular, that Alki was exposed to winds from the north as well as the south, that vessels could be blown ashore and logs blown away and that he had chosen a very poor site for his mill.

Renton's California associates tired of the business and returned to San Francisco, but Renton didn't give up. He interested another San Francisco acquaintance of his, Daniel S. Howard, in joining him in the enterprise.

The two men formed a new partnership in 1854, and moved the mill machinery from Alki to Port Orchard, the name given by Captain Vancouver to what he thought was a long inlet on the west side of Bainbridge Island. Lt. Wilkes later determined that the "long inlet" was a navigable waterway between what Wilkes named Bainbridge Island and the mainland to the west. The mill site was on the west side of the waterway and somewhat more protected than Alki, but it had its drawbacks, too. One of them was that it proved difficult for ships to reach. Speaking years later about getting to the mill in the 1860s, a Captain W. B. Seymore recalled, "We then made sail again from Seattle, so unimportant a town that no one cared to go ashore, crossed the Sound and worked our way up through Port Orchard Narrows, and quite a little task too, to the mill at Port Orchard, which was located about a mile north of (the future) Manette.".

In 1855, shortly after the formation of the new partnership, and probably triggered by the expenses of the move to the new location, Renton and Howard ran into financial difficulty. Those difficulties were recalled by Howard's brother, Captain Edward Howard of San Francisco.

> I took the bark *Leonisa* to Puget Sound, taking my brother, Dan, Captain Renton and a Mr. Theodore as passengers. My brother and Captain Renton were the owners of a sawmill at Port Orchard, but they had run in debt and had mortgaged the mill property. A man named Washington Loomis had jumped the claim, mill and all. I had to buy him off and settled the other claims and started the mill going. I waited until they had cut a cargo of lumber, which I loaded in the bark and sent down to San Francisco. But the detention and other expenses had been so great that I lost money by the venture.

Perhaps to do what he could to recoup his investment, Captain Howard settled near the mill.

> I then took up 350 acres of land at Port Orchard and built a nice cottage and laid out a garden; bought some cows, sheep and hogs; goats I had brought from Calcutta. Started a chicken ranch, but the skunks killed the chickens and the Indian dogs killed the sheep. My wife could not stand the continual worries, besides the loneliness, so we decided when the bark returned to

sell the remainder of the stock at a great sacrifice, and deserted the place and came down in the bark to San Francisco.

Difficult working and living conditions weren't all that early settlers had to contend with. Sometimes their personal safety was at risk during native uprisings. One story was told of Captain Renton returning to Port Orchard from Olympia by Indian canoe during the native uprising of the 1850s. His loyal paddlers put the cargo blankets over Renton when their canoe was approached by unfriendly Indians. The trip was safely finished and in appreciation Renton is said to have built some "white man's" housing for the Indians employed at the mill, but the Indians are believed never to have used them. Renton's relations with his Indian employees were unusually good, and the canoe incident tends to confirm this.

In spite of the Indians and the "continual worries" encountered by Mrs. Howard, Sarah Renton and her girls sometimes joined Renton at Port Orchard, probably for summer visits, from their winter home in San Francisco.

During one of these summer visits a romance blossomed, and the oldest of the girls, Mary Ann, married David Livingston, a mill employee. Their wedding was in Olympia on August 17, 1857. That was the bright side of the year.

The dark side was nearly fatal. There was a boiler explosion at the mill, and Renton was struck in the forehead by a heavy piece of metal. The accident severely injured Renton, and resulted in his being plagued by repeated headaches and, later, by the loss of his sight.

On June 2, 1858, Mary Ann and David presented the Rentons with Sarah's first grandchild, Clara Martha Livingston. She is believed to have been the first white child born at Port Orchard. There were probably other bright sides to life there, but sadness and discouragement never seemed far away. Sarah's daughter, Josephine, died this year in San Francisco. Most of the small group of non-Indian employees probably agreed with Captain Howard's assessment of living conditions, or with the following assessment by David Mills, the young engineer at the mill. Mills' remarks are contained in a letter to his brother, James, in Scotland.

September 28, 1861
Port Orchard, Washington Territory

Dear Brother,

I received your letter and was glad to hear from you. I would have wrote you sooner, but I got out of work in San Francisco. I was 2 or 3 weeks idle, then my brother in law (his wife's sister's husband, Captain Dan Howard) gave me the offer to go up to the saw mill to drive the engine. I accepted, and I have been driving her here now for 10 months, and I like it pretty well, but this place is very dull. It is about 890 miles further away than San Francisco. Our fare costs us nothing traveling on this side of the world, because my brother in law is half owner in the mill, and they own a large bark called the *Nahumkeag*, which we travel on free of expenses. We keep 3 vessels sailing all the time between this and Frisco, carrying away the lumber.

But now to give you an idea of the place we live in, it is the greatest country of timber that ever was known, and bushes such that you can not walk through 10 yards off the beach. The loggers when they go to work in the woods commence to make a road for themselves from the river side. They draw the logs with oxen into the water and make a large raft of logs of 4 and 5 hundred, and bring them to the mill with the tide. This river is called Puget Sound. It is about 200 miles long. We are about 180 miles up, ourselves, that is from the Pacific Ocean. Some parts of the sound is 4 miles wide, some parts 2 miles.

There is only 6 white men employed in the mill, and there is 5 Indians employed in the mill for carrying away the slabs and taking the lumber down to the wharf. This is the natives of this country. They are strange people. Their skin is a very dark copper color and they wear very long hair down their back and their heads is flat on the back side and the front side. This is done to them all after they are born. They have articles that they screw on them which is made of wood. They can speak no English at all. Neither can they learn to speak it. All the clothing they wear is a single blanket, and very lazy inclined.

All they live on is clams and fish, mussels and venison. There is any quantity of them living up and down here. You could not tell a man from a woman to look at them. Men have no beards. Any of them that have any hair on their face pull it out so that it do not grow. An Indian will only work a day or so at a time, and they change among themselves. I have got pretty good now to talk their language myself. They never get any learning, neither are they taught anything. They are very wild in general, but round here they are pretty civil.

I have here a free house, fire and light board. We have a cookhouse here for the mill, and all the mill hands eat in it. My pay is 3 pounds 10 shillings a week in English money, that is 17 and a half dollars in Californian money. There is only 5 houses here of white people. We have a nice little house ourselves, with 4 fine rooms. All the rest are single men except the other owner. He lives here.

I came up here myself first for 2 months, then the family came up. I have got to be temperate here, whether I will or not. There is no drink here nor within 100 miles of us. I expect to see you all in the course of 2 years, when I save a trifle worth while to come home with.

I must draw to a close, as the vessel is about to sail. Agnes and the children is well. Catherine is got to be a very large girl, likewise Willie. He is a very wild boy. Give my love to Alexander and wife and family, William and wife and all their family, and David and Margaret, and all enquiring friends. Be sure and write when you receive this, and address the letter the same as you did before. I have forgot the address myself. I will give you more news when I write next. No more at present.

I remain your loving brother
David Mills

Besides giving a feeling for the remoteness of Port Orchard, David Mills' letter suggests how few people there were on Puget Sound and how often the few families on its shores were related. David Mills had been married in Scotland to Agnes Smith in 1857. That was three years after Renton had entered into partnership with Daniel Howard, whose wife, Elizabeth, was Agnes Mills' sister.

Renton turned forty-three in 1861. He had persevered for eight years in his efforts to start a successful lumber milling enterprise, but now returned to California, apparently quite depressed with its future prospects. Some say he intended to give

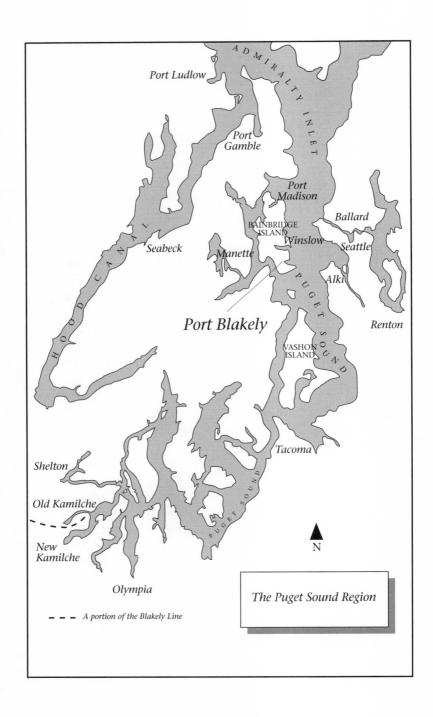

Port Ludlow

Port Gamble

Port Madison

Ballard

BAINBRIDGE ISLAND

Winslow

Seattle

Seabeck

Manette

Alki

ADMIRALTY INLET

HOOD CANAL

Port Blakely

Renton

VASHON ISLAND

PUGET SOUND

Tacoma

Shelton

Old Kamilche

New Kamilche

PUGET SOUND

N

Olympia

The Puget Sound Region

– – – *A portion of the Blakely Line*

up, and this seems to be supported by Snowden, who, writing in 1909, speaks of the sale in 1862 of the Port Orchard mill to James M. Colman and N. H. Falk.

Renton's step son-in-law, David Livingston, must have shared the impression that Captain Renton was quitting Puget Sound, for in 1863 Livingston was on the Snohomish River where he built a small sawmill about three miles above its mouth.

Renton stayed in San Francisco for several months and recouped his energy, but he couldn't shake the idea of how profitable a successful mill on Puget Sound might be. In 1863, he went searching again, and near the southeast end of Bainbridge Island he found the site he'd been looking for — Blakely Harbor. The oft repeated story is that he and Theodore Williams plumbed the harbor depth with a clothes line and determined that it was deep enough for ocean-going, lumber-laden sailing ships.

෧

CHAPTER THREE

THE FIRST MILL AT PORT BLAKELY IS BUILT, DIFFICULT DAYS ARE SURVIVED, THE CAMPBELL BROTHERS ARRIVE

Captain Renton was not the first man who was taken with deep, three-quarters of a mile long Blakely Harbor. The Indians were there first, of course. And British Captain George Vancouver came close, but instead of ducking into the harbor, he spent his time exploring Port Orchard and upper Puget Sound from an anchorage on the south side of Restoration Point. Then came American Lieutenant Charles Wilkes, commander of the United States Exploring Expedition, who named the harbor.

Its naming was recorded by George T. Sinclair, the acting master of the *Porpoise*, one of the ships of the United States Exploring Expedition. On Monday, May 31, 1841, Sinclair wrote in his log: "At half past one p.m. got under way and at half past four anchored outside the outer harbor of Port Orchard on the east side of Bainbridge Island near the mouths of two very fine little harbors, one of which we called Eagle Harbor and the other, a southern one, Blakely Harbor in honor of the memory of the brave officer of that name who was killed in the last war."

Later, Reuben Bean, a pioneer from Kennebec County, Maine, agreed with Sinclair that the southern harbor was indeed "very fine." Bean settled a claim on Blakely Harbor on January 20, 1854. His was the first homestead on the harbor, and his

148.5 acres reached from the south side of Blakely Harbor across to the south side of the island to what is still known as Bean's Bight and South Beach.

Like Renton, Bean may have seen the potential of the lumber industry in the Northwest. The two men traveled in the same circles, and in fact, Daniel Howard and George Washington Loomis witnessed Bean's claim document. Of course, that was some months before Daniel's brother, Edward, rescued Daniel and Renton from Loomis' clutches. Renton, Howard, Bean and Loomis had likely known each other almost from the week of their arrival on the central part of the Sound. Lumber, lumber mills and ships were part of every conversation, and undoubtedly Bean knew of Renton's difficulties at Alki and his search for a new site.

Bean was prescient, but nine years premature. He was killed in 1859, supposedly by Indians. Part of his property was eventually acquired by Captain Renton's Port Blakely Mill Company, and another part became known as Ryderville, a real thorn in the side of the company that owned most everything else on the harbor.

It may have taken Renton longer than Bean to recognize the suitability of Blakely Harbor as a mill site, but when he finally did, he lost no time. On June 30, 1863, Renton filed for the land on which the mill was to be built. He started by purchasing the five government lots that make up the inner part of the harbor. They totaled 164.5 acres and gave him control of the majority of the "low bank", level land around the harbor. He was able to buy the 160 acres he was entitled to under the Donation Land Act for $1.25 an acre with $10.00 down. He had to pay the full price in cash for the additional 4.5 acres over his Land Act entitlement. That came to $5.63 more. During the twelve months after Renton's first purchase of land, he bought five more parcels on higher ground, 80 acres to the south of the harbor and 160 acres to the north. The stream that became the mills most important water source ran through the 160 acre parcel and into the head of the harbor from the northwest.

The Blakely Harbor mill site was just four miles due east of the mill at Port Orchard and four and one half miles northwest of his original site on Alki Point, but it was infinitely better suited to his purposes than either of the first two locations. It had an adequate water supply close at hand and easy to develop, and had substantially more flat ground on which a sawmill and the necessary company town could be built. The inner harbor would provide a good log storage and sorting area. The former locations had neither. The outer harbor was deep enough to accommodate several ships of the size needed to carry lumber to market. The surrounding hills gave protection from the north and south winds of summer and winter and from the occasional storm winds that blew in from the west. And still the site was within three-quarters of a mile of the open Sound.

The initial job was to clear the site of the virgin timber that covered it. Simultaneously, Renton surveyed the site to see exactly where to locate the sawmill structure and how best to place it. Other men worked to turn the stream at the head of the harbor into a water source with sufficient head to feed the mills boilers and serve the new community. Others planned and erected the buildings to house and feed the men who would run the mill. Lumber for them may have been brought from Port Orchard, but Renton's desire to get into production meant that every nonproductive structure was pretty primitive.

The sawmill was built on fir piling driven into the water, the beach and the north shore of the harbor. The piles were gathered on the site during land clearing. Some supported the heavy boilers, steam engines, log carriages and saws. Some, those driven into the beaches and below the low tide line, supported wharves on which green lumber was stacked and from which ships were loaded. Some were driven in deeper water to form a saltwater "pen" or holding area for saw logs.

The original mill is said to have had a capacity of between 20,000 and 30,000 board feet a day. The equipment needed to deliver that capacity came from San Francisco. It was assembled by the mill crew—there were no specialized contractors in those days.

Construction was finished in April 1864. The mill steamed up, and the new equipment came to life with David Mills again the engineer and part of the twenty-man payroll. On May 28, the *Nahumkeag*, presumably named by its first owner for the grassy salt marshes along Cape Cod Bay in Massachusetts, the company ship commanded by Captain I. W. Gove, arrived and began loading the first cargo of lumber shipped from the new town that was soon named Port Blakely.

Early lithographs and photographs of the sawmill show that it had a long ridged roof with three diamond shaped windows at each end and more such windows on the side. Logs were stored in the water beside the mill and taken into it from the west end. There was no waste or sawdust burner; continuous chains or belts carried waste out onto open burn piles.

Renton seems to have been too busy during his first two years on Blakely Harbor to write his mother, but he wrote in the Spring of 1866 and condensed those first two years into the following letter. It is the initial letter of ten which survive and cover the period from 1866 to 1873.

May 12, 1866

Dear Mother,

It is with pleasure that I take my pen in hand to write you, hoping this may find you and my sisters enjoying good health, as it leaves me, thank the giver of all good. I would have

---

The 1863 mill as it appeared in about 1880, Port Blakely, Washington Territory. Lithograph courtesy University of Washington, Special Collections, 2916.

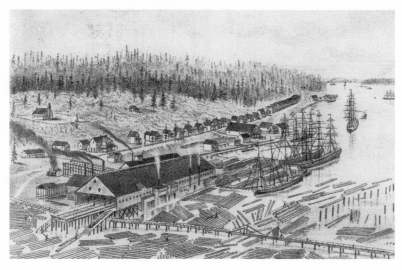

Captain Renton circa 1866. Photo courtesy Museum of History and Industry.

written before, but a man from Pictou by the name of McDonald just returned from there and working at a mill on the sound has been sending word that he had seen you and my sisters and was coming to see me to deliver a message, but he has failed to come with whatever message you may have sent me.

I was in hopes to have gone home this summer to see you, but business has been so very dull for the six months just past, and (sic) have built a new mill which we thought would cost us not more than $25,000, but it has cost us over $50,000 and not quite finished yet. And to help matters my partner died at the time that his assistance was most valuable to me. He attended to the San Francisco end of the business and was a valuable man. He was thrown from a buggy and had both legs broken, and mortification set in which soon ended his earthly troubles. His loss threw the whole on me and I have had a trying time of it. But I have got things in pretty good working shape and hope to be able to leave next spring for a visit to you.

My wife has gone to San Francisco. Will be back in a few weeks. She has assisted me very much in my troubles. Josephine is dead. Elizabeth is a widow with two boys, Joseph W. and William Renton Phillips. She is going to Philadelphia on a visit and may extend her visit to you. She resides in San Francisco, and her mother has gone to see her before she leaves.

Mary Ann is here. Her husband, David Livingston, is foreman of the mill. She has three children: Clara, Josephine and George W. Livingston.

Enclosed you will find my photograph taken about one year ago.

Give my kind regards to my sisters and all my relatives.
Hoping to hear from you soon,

I remain your affect. son

W. Renton

When you write, address William Renton, Port Blakely,
Puget Sound, Washington Territory.

Mary Ann and her husband send their love to you all.

The village on Blakely Harbor was now called Port Blakely.
A simple address—no numbers—just Port Blakely, Puget Sound,
Washington Territory. Perhaps because business in 1866 was "so
very dull", Renton found time to write to his mother again on
September 24. It's hard to imagine a more comprehensive letter.
His mother must have felt completely caught up by the time she
finished it. I wonder what she thought of her "little boy".

Blakely Mill, September 24, 1866

My Dear Mother,

I rec'd yours of July 20. It was over two months in coming. I had almost given up of hearing from you, and I assure you
I was much pleased when your letter arrived. It links me with my
friends again. I wish I could leave here and go see you and my
sisters, but I hope that providence will favor me so that I can go
next summer.

You did not mention Elizabeth or James. You must have
forgotten them, but I see sister Mary has not forgotten any of us
in naming her numerous family. I hope her children will be a
comfort to her. I would like very much to see my namesake. I can
only look back and see my sisters as children, as they were when
I left home, not as women with streaks of grey in their locks.

My own locks are getting white and my head is somewhat
bald. I am not the little boy I was when I left home, but weigh
about 250. So you see I am no chicken for size.

Sarah returned from San Francisco about two months ago.
Lizzie did not go east on account of the cholera being there, but
likely will next spring.

Mary Ann, husband and family are well. Josephine died
about eight years ago with consumption.

I have been settled here since fifty three. Howard, my partner that died, was a native of London, England. He was a good man and attended to the business in San Francisco. He attended the yard and I the mill. After his death the widow sold his interest to Messrs. Preston and McKennon, the latter a native of P. E. Island. He came up to see me to arrange matters, and when he returned to Frisco, she backed out because she could get something more than they had agreed to give. Which was the beginning of my troubles. Had they got the mill I have no doubt things would have went well, but we must take the world as it comes. No doubt all is for the best, although it does not always appear so to us poor mortals.

The parties that got the widows interest cannot manage matters, and I think we will have to separate in some way. Hope I can make them buy me out, for I am getting tired of this wooden country.

About making money in this country: Some make, but others do not. In looking around I see that all do make that are industrious, sober and attend to there business. Liquor is the great curse of this country, as it is of every other, and it is the greatest source of trouble I have to contend with. Men are scarce, wages high and they spend there (sic) earnings recklessly. The day will come when things will be different, but it will be some time.

First, laborers wages range from $30 to $50 per month and sound mechanics from $65 to $250; the latter is an extreme figure. Millwrights and engineers usually get $100 to $125 per month.

With board, a family can live very cheap here. No wood or water to buy and provisions cheap: Flour $8 per bbl, beef 10c, sugar 14c, tea and coffee 33 1/3c, potatoes 37 1/2c per bushel, other things in proportion. It costs us 35c per day per man to board the men in the cook house. That is the actual cost.

We have from 30 to 40 men around the mill. The total monthly expense, including logs, is about $5000. We usually saw from 30M to 40M ft per day of twelve hours.

Don't understand me that I advise any person to leave fair business to come here, and I would not advise any person to come, for the country is very wild; no schools, few churches and them poorly attended. Laws that cannot be enforced for the want of good men for policemen.

When I was in Frisco about two years ago I called on a Mr. David McKay, a wholesale dealer in groceries and provisions, thinking I might know him, but I did not. He belongs to a tribe of the McKays that I did not know in Pictou. He told me of a Mr. Joseph Gordon that resided in San Francisco, a native of Pictou also, but I did not see him and I think if I recollect aright, John Gordon's brother was David, although McKay made Joseph Gordon a brother of Captain John Gordon. Said the brother of the Gordons was a Scotsman and kept a store in Pictou.

Years ago, Mother, you used to tell me you had me marked with that scar got when out in the woods with Mr. Thomas Patterson and brother James. But you would not know me by it now, as our mill was blown up some seven years ago and I was severely injured about the head and face, and that scar has considerably enlarged. But still does not show much, but if you remember the old scar you would not know me by the one I have now.

I held this back a week, thinking that I could send you news of my coming at an early day. I expect to sell my interest in the mill, but so far have not succeeded. Will send you some photographs as soon as we get some place where we can get these taken. Remember we live in the woods.

Sarah, Mary Ann and husband send their love to you and sisters.

I remain your Affectionate son, W. Renton

The somber notes he strikes with his hope that the parties that bought out the interest of Daniel Howard's widow will soon buy him out, "for I am getting tired of this wooden country", and "I expect to sell my interest in the mill and come and see you" are ones he repeats in several letters.

In April 1867 he wrote:

I am in hopes to sell out this summer, when we will pay you a visit. Business is improving. When it gets good there will be no trouble in selling. About half of the mills failed in the last two years, but I think the worst is over. Business is much better than it was, and I think it will be very good this summer. At all events prospects are very good at present.

Another view of the first mill at Port Blakely, 1882. Photo courtesy University of Washington, Special Collections, Watkins 5251.

Our losses last year by failures was very heavy. In fact the lumber trade is losing its attraction for me. I would rather try something else.

In August 1867 he wrote:

In a few days I leave for San Francisco in hopes of being able to sell my interest in the mill while business is good, for I do not want to pass through another two years like the two just passed. Every thing on this coast is overdone. You either make money very fast or lose fast. There is no such thing as a steady paying business. Everything goes by extremes. People live fast and appear never to think of the morrow.
If I can sell out, Martha and I will pay you a visit.

Sometimes Renton referred to his wife as Sarah, sometimes as Martha. In another letter, in September, he seemed positive his days on Puget Sound were over, for on the 18th he wrote:

> You had better not write until you hear from me again as in all likelihood I will sell out my interest in Puget Sound and may take up my residence in San Francisco or return to the Atlantic States. But I will write you as soon as matters and things are settled.

But then in April of 1868, the negative is mixed with a positive tone.

> The partnership will not expire before January 1st, 1870, and my partners object to my selling. I thought they would buy my interest, but it takes so much money that they cannot buy at present. But I hope they will this fall. They make the promise at all events.
>
> We have been very busy this year. So far have shipped five million since 1st January, and have five vessels in port now. Three of our own: the *Sampson* carrying 750 M, the *Nicholas Biddle* 600M, and *Leamore* 300M. One English Bk to load for Callao and the *Gem of the Ocean* loading for Frisco. You can judge by that that I have very little leisure time.
>
> Business has been very good for the last eight months, with every prospect of continuing for some time. We are running night and day cutting about 70M average every twenty four hours. We go on the principal 'make hay while the sun shines'.

Renton seems delighted to be making money so fast and also to have forgotten his observation that "Everything on this coast is overdone". In several letters he refers to sending money to his mother, usually in the form of drafts purchased in Victoria for payment in Pictou. And in these letters from Port Blakely he always uses Martha in referring to his wife, not Sarah.

Renton wrote his mother again in August, 1868. There is nothing special about this letter, but it may have been the last one Margaret Renton received from her son, for she died in February of 1869 at age seventy-eight. Margaret and Adam are buried in the Renton family plot at Haliburton Cemetery just outside of Pictou. A substantial inscribed obelisk marks the plot.

The last three surviving letters were written to Renton's brother-in-law, William Campbell. The Campbell family came to Nova Scotia from Red Castle, Rossshire, Scotland. One son, John had been born in Red Castle in 1815. William was born in Pictou in 1828. The two brothers grew up in Pictou. A close friendship developed between the Campbells and the Rentons, and later on John Campbell married Captain Renton's sister Mary and William married his sister Margaret.

William and Margaret Renton Campbell had no children, but as an earlier letter indicates, John and Mary did- three sons and two daughters. Captain Renton and Sarah had no children of their own, so it was natural for Renton to feel especially close to his nephews. By 1872 two of the boys, John A. and William had joined their uncle at Port Blakely to work in his sawmill, and the next letter to Nova Scotia gives a progress report on the boys. John was about twenty-five and William about eighteen. Since the letter, written in November 1872, was written to William, not the boys' father John, even though the boys' parents were still in Pictou, it suggests that Renton probably wrote one time to John and the next time to William, and that the letters to John have been lost.

Renton wrote that "the boys are well. John would be a favorite anywhere. They have both done remarkably well, and I am very pleased with them." About four months later, in March 1873, he wrote again, "John and Will is well and steady as ever. I feel proud of them; they are so steady and well behaved that they are both universally liked."

The last letter that has been found was written to William about seven months later on October 25, 1873. By this time Renton was better acquainted with his nephews. The pertinent part of this last letter follows:

> Enclosed you will find a photo of Tacoma, the western terminus of the North (sic) Pacific RR for the present. John and Will are determined to have terminus property, having bought lots at Seattle and Tacoma. They are likely to strike right somewhere. For my own part, I don't think much of Tacoma, although they may make something out of it if they can find a bottom in the bay.
>
> John and Will is well. The latter is assistant engineer on the boat, and if he will stick to it he will make engineer in time. He is fickle; don't like anything long. John is the steady old fel-

low—always on hand and always the same. He is the most even tempered man that I ever met with. Don't think he ever gets out of humor. Remember, I don't speak disparagingly of Will. He is doing well, but John is a rare man, one that is not often met with.

Both boys worked first as apprentice machinists at the sawmill, although William's interests soon caused him to leave the mill to turn engineer on steamboats and steam tugs. John measured up to his uncle's assessment and played a more important role in the Port Blakely operations each year.

No more letters are known to have survived. Fortunately, the ones that have cover the early years at Port Blakely and carry Renton into the period of prosperity that started only after he had been in the business on Puget Sound for nearly twenty years.

ð

CHAPTER FOUR

CHARLES S. HOLMES JOINS THE FIRM IN SAN FRANCISCO, MANAGEMENT CHANGES IN PORT BLAKELY

As Renton wrote in his first letter from Port Blakely, his partner, Dan Howard, died just as the Port Blakely enterprise was getting going. Sometime shortly before his death in the summer of 1863, Howard hired a clerk to work with him in the San Francisco sales office on Stewart Street at Pier 3. The clerk, recently arrived from Foxcroft, Maine, was Charles S. Holmes. Holmes became a tower of strength for Renton, ultimately succeeding to the presidency of the company.

Shortly after Howard's death, a man named Samuel E. Smith took charge of the San Francisco office. Later, in 1867, the name of the company, which had been Renton and Howard, was changed to Renton, Smith and Company. The partners brought in Richard K. Ham, a bachelor, to be a part of the enterprise. He came from Stafford County, New Hampshire, where he was born August 3, 1821. Like Renton, who was three years his senior, he became a sea captain. He arrived in San Francisco as captain of the ship *Capitol* on July 19, 1849, about a year ahead of Renton. Four years later, in 1853, he owned a fleet of seven lumber "coasters"and was considered a rich man. He settled in Santa Clara in August of 1853, and entered the "livery" business, while continuing the ownership of his lumber "coaster" fleet. Ham seems to have been a "silent partner", but his financial participation was substantial and the association between Renton and Ham was a lasting one.

San Francisco grew very rapidly during the 1860s. Lumber for homes could usually be marketed profitably as quickly as it reached the city. The mill at Port Blakely prospered, and so did the town. Proud of them both, sawmill engineer David Mills and his wife, Agnes, named their son, born on November 9, 1867, Blakely Mills. He was the first white baby born in Port Blakely.

The census for 1870 reveals that there were fifty-nine Caucasians and a few Indians living in Port Blakely. Among the newcomers, there were five families besides the Mills. Bigelow and Christian Longfellow arrived from Maine with their two children. The bookkeeper of the mill was Oliver McCausland, who, with his wife, Addie, came from Canada. William and Mary Nelson were immigrants from Denmark, and Thomas Wellington, an immigrant from England, lived with his four-year-old son, Charlie, who had been born in Washington Territory.

Reading the countries of origin of these families and the single men listed in the same census makes it clear that Port Blakely was a town of immigrants. Most of them were young. The foreign-born adults numbered thirty-four and were twice as numerous as the American-born adults who numbered sixteen. Of the foreign-born, three came from eastern Canada; nineteen in all from England, Scotland and Ireland. Two each came from Denmark, Norway and Sweden. Two came from France, two from Prussia, one from Belgium and one from Greece. Sort of a western Babel!

Of the American-born adults, six came from Maine, four from Massachusetts and two from New York. Four other states were represented. All nine of the children in the community appear to have had English-speaking parents.

Renton had houses built for the families he employed and dormitories for the men. For some of the senior men, there were six two-room cabins.

All of this early development was on the north side of Blakely harbor. Captain Renton's house was closest to the mill. The dormitories were west of his house near the mill pond. Other houses were built along the shore to the east of Renton's house. In front of them ran Bay Street, partly on solid ground, partly on planks supported by pilings driven into the beach.

There is no mention of a hotel keeper in the census although a county census a year later showed that Pat Sherry and his wife, June, held this position. If it was true that David Mills couldn't get a drink within 100 miles of Port Orchard, and that was obviously an exaggeration, that wasn't true in Port Blakely in 1870. Richard King was identified in the census as "retail liquor dealer". The census also recorded the name of a visiting business man, a Mr. Legrand Morehead, quite a highfalutin' name for a small town of Rentons, Mills and the like. In the census, Morehead is listed as "manufacturer of lumber", and the census suggests he was a man of means.

The so-called resident proprietor of the sawmill in 1868 had been Mr. M. R. Smith. One wonders if he was related to Renton's new partner, Samuel E. Smith. In 1869, Smith's wife arrived in town and she must have persuaded him to give a high priority to opening a school. According to an early account, "he exerted himself to have a school established and have the town made a desirable place for men with families". Despite his exertions, Smith proved not to be the mill manager Renton wanted: by the time of the 1870 census, the Smith family had gone. There is no record of whether or not Mr. Smith was successful in establishing a school, but the town's first recognized public school, Kitsap County School District No. 5's Port Blakely School, wasn't founded until 1876.

The Renton family wasn't in that census either, which may be the best commentary on life during Bainbridge Island frontier days. The rough-and-tumble life must have been especially hard on Mrs. Renton. Renton maintained a home in San Francisco to which she could go for extended visits. In contrast to a place where mud, smoke and buzzing saws were the overwhelming characteristics, the Renton's San Francisco address was the rather elegant-sounding 111 St. Marks Place.

Seattle of the 1860s offered little more to Sarah Renton and the other residents of Port Blakely than it did to Captain W. B. Seymore's crew, which found it "so unimportant." The business section of the town was confined to the two blocks on Commercial Street south from Yesler Way. The forest came down to the University building between what are now Fourth and Seventh Avenues, and everything north of Madison Street was recently logged-off land. In all, about 2,000 people lived in Seattle at the end of the decade. All travel to and from the town was by boat, and there was still a fear that commercial supremacy might pass the city by, leaving it stranded as a forest-hidden boat landing.

As would be expected in a frontier town whose population swelled each time a ship pulled in, crime was no stranger to Port Blakely. The murder of Edward James Butler, a native of Ireland and mate on the British bark *Marinus*, was a particularly bloody one. Butler had a standing quarrel with John R. Smith, a stevedore and occasional pilot of the *Marinus*.

The quarrel escalated into a shouting match on April 28, 1868, while the ship was loading lumber at Port Blakely. Butler yelled at Smith to part the lines; Smith yelled back at Butler; Butler retaliated by calling Smith a "son-of-a-bitch". Smith waited for the perfect time, which came when Butler was leaning on the railing of the ship, yelling orders to the men below. Smith hefted a large capstan rod and let Butler have what court records of the day called a "mortal blow to the back of the head". Butler's hat fell over the railing as he began to fall; Smith hit him another "mortal" blow on the front of the head, and the mate lay on the deck. "He didn't say a word," a witness in court said of Butler.

Smith dropped the rod and ran for shore, hurrying to Captain Renton's house to ask for a bottle of camphor to use on a man who was "about killed," Mrs. Renton reported to the court later. "He feared the man would die. I asked him who did it. He pointed to himself".

Smith returned to the ship, accompanied by Captain Renton, but after one look Renton told him it was no use, Butler was dead.

The next day a jury of six men was called by B. E. Lambard, justice of the peace and acting coroner. There were several witnesses to the crime, and they all testified that Smith had indeed killed Butler. Smith himself pled guilty and was taken to jail at Steilacoom.

And there were other crimes. A notorious pair of outlaws

was convicted of robbery late in the 1860s. George Bargeman and Daniel Brown already had a record: they were convicted of petty theft for stealing a "tin pan worth 75-cents and two dozen eggs worth 50-cents each" from a lady's house in Port Blakely. Another time they took some pantaloons, gold pieces, two hats, a pair of boots and some suspenders from a port resident's house and were caught red-handed. The third time they took more pantaloons, money and a knife from another resident. The knife was found on Bargeman, and the ne'er-do-wells were again thrown in jail.

It's not hard to understand why Mrs. Renton preferred San Francisco.

ह&

CHAPTER FIVE

THE PACE PICKS UP
AND PORT BLAKELY COMES
OF AGE—THE 1870s

Port Blakely was one of many small sawmill towns on Puget Sound at the beginning of the 1870s. Port Madison on the same island was larger, as were Port Gamble and Seabeck on Hood Canal. The men who were running the mills in each of those communities expected to be successful, or in today's idiom, "to be a survivor". Being successful required the right blend of resources, production, marketing, financing and human skills that has always been necessary in any successful endeavor of size. Of the early starters in sawmilling on lower Puget Sound and Hood Canal, the operators of the mills at Port Blakely and at Port Gamble stood out. They found the right blend.

At the beginning of the decade, Captain Renton and his family were living in San Francisco rather than Port Blakely. In the Captain's absence, the acting manager of the mill was Oliver J. McCausland, formerly the mill's bookkeeper. There was a temporary suspension of mill production in the summer of 1870 precipitated by the breakdown of the company's steam tug, *Columbia*. The *Columbia* was expected back in service during October, but shutdowns, no matter for what reason, resulted in poor service to customers, and that couldn't be tolerated. So Renton, fifty-two and with poor eyesight, returned. He and Sarah

Another view of the first mill at Port Blakely, 1882. Photo courtesy University of Washington, Special Collections, Watkins 5237.

were in Port Blakely at the time of the 1871 Kitsap County census, which still lists Renton's occupation as "Shipmaster".

In spite of McCausland's problems, the port was not idle: down the shore from the mill, Oliver Engblom, also known as Ole, was about to launch the fourteen-ton schooner *Ontario*. Two years earlier, in 1869, he had launched the 104-foot, 253 ton topsail schooner *Alice Haake* for J. C. Haake & Co. and two years later, in 1872, he launched the 176-ton steam tug *Blakely* for the mill company—probably to replace the troublesome *Columbia*. Also built on the harbor in 1872 was the 206 ton schooner *Serena Thayer*. At the docks in September, the *John Day* was loading piling for San Francisco, and the *Nicholas Biddle* and the *Oak Hill* were loading lumber for the same port.

Lumber production capacity at the mill moved up from 70,000 board feet each day in 1868 toward 90,000 board feet per day in 1870. More ships called at the wharves to move this production to distant markets. Most were not owned by the company.

A major communications improvement became available in 1871 when the mill at Port Blakely was connected by telegraph to the Renton, Smith & Co. office in San Francisco. What

Company houses, the new Bainbridge Hotel, and in the distance Hall Brothers Shipyard. Photo courtesy University of Washington, Special Collections, Watkins 5245.

a welcome improvement that must have been for all aspects of the management of the firm, perhaps most importantly for the sales department. Renton was a founding investor in the Puget Sound Telegraph Company that made the service possible, and he was one of its directors.

Samuel E. Smith, Captain Renton's partner of about five years, died in 1873 in San Francisco. Renton explained this loss in his letter of October 25, 1873 to his brother-in-law William Campbell:

> I suppose the boys have informed you of the death of my partner, Mr. Smith, by falling down a ship hold. He fell into the hold of the vessel *Carrier Dove*. My former partner, Captain Howard, was killed by being thrown out of a buggy against a gas post, so you see that I am very unfortunate with partners.
>
> This last was very unfortunate for we were just getting the business in fine working shape and Mr. Smith was getting well posted in his end, and altogether we were getting things in better shape than we ever had it before. It will be very hard to replace him.

The language Renton used in referring to Smith in this letter and to Howard in his May 1866 letter convey the impression that both were trustworthy businessmen truly important to the success of the enterprise. Fortunately, Charles S. Holmes, who had worked for Howard and for Smith in the San Francisco office, was excellently equipped to carry on.

Port Blakely was looking toward a prosperous future, but it was not isolated from the economy of the Sound, the coast or the world beyond. The entire Pacific Northwest breathed what turned out to be a premature sigh of relief when the Northern Pacific Railway finally reached Tacoma from Kalama on the Columbia River on December 16, 1873. The line was connected by railroad barge with the main line at Portland, so passengers should have been able to make the transcontinental journey to Puget Sound completely by train. This was such an important event, that some later historians suggested that December 16, 1873, should signal the end of the "pioneer period."

However, even though the Pacific Northwest portion of the tracks had been laid, work on the railroad from the east had come to a stop clear back in Bismarck, North Dakota. Confidence in the financial markets had collapsed in September of 1873, after a scandal was exposed that involved the recently completed Union Pacific. The scandal was given the name "Credit Mobilier." Jay Cooke, whose banking house had sold the bonds that financed the Northern Pacific, could sell no more, and his firm failed. Eventually, the railroad was completed but not for another ten years.

The nationwide collapse of the financial markets caused the demand for lumber in California to fall to not much more than could be supplied from inventory at the mill company's San Francisco yards on Pier 3 off Stewart Street. The mill in Port Blakely was virtually shut down.

In spite of the depressed market, the mill that had cost Renton more than $50,000 in 1864 had sales of $1.5 million ten years later in 1874, and a year later the economy recovered to the point that the mill company added to its ownership of timberlands. In a letter to Holmes in San Francisco, Renton wrote, "We purchased land last week for $4,000. There is some 15 to 20 million board feet on it, enough to last for several years."

Bainbridge Hotel. Photo courtesy University of Washington, Special Collections, Dorsaz & Schwerin 12327.

What an exciting time the last few years had been. Between 1870 and 1874, the population of San Francisco had grown by 51,000 people to over 200,000. The majority of homes, including the elegant Nob Hill homes, had been built of wood—much of it from Port Blakely. It had been a bonanza for the owners of the mill.

Ole Engblom's shipyard was taken over by W. H. Bryant, who launched three ships there during 1874. The largest of the ships was built for the mill, the 569-ton barkentine *R.K. Ham*, named for Renton's partner. Its skipper was I.W. Gove, the captain of the company's first ship, the *Nahumkeag,* and a longtime captain of other sailing and steam vessels on the Sound. The *R.K. Ham* made over 100 trips between Puget Sound and San Francisco, all under Captain Gove, before being wrecked on the Dungeness Spit in August, 1894. The two smaller ships to come off the ways at Bryant's yard in Port Blakely were the 232-ton schooner *Alice* and the 200-ton schooner *Una*.

On July 11, 1875, a new partnership, Renton, Holmes and Co., was formed. Renton and his "silent" partner, Richard K. Ham, had decided to take Charles S. Holmes into the business as a partner. Of course, that was a two-way street—Holmes must have been satisfied that Renton and Ham ran a business with which he wanted to be associated as an investor as well as an employee. Few people could have known the company better.

He had been with Renton for ten years, first as a clerk, then as a bookkeeper. He was forty-one and Renton was fifty-five. Holmes proved as able a businessman as both Renton and Ham.

A fine new hotel was built in 1875, replacing one that had become grossly inadequate. The main building was 30 feet by 200 feet. It was two stories in height and had a porch facing Bay Street and a balcony. A 30 foot by 60 foot one story service building was located behind the main building. The new gleaming white Bainbridge Hotel gave Port Blakely class. Now it was really a place to write home about.

The hotel had seventy-five rooms, in a town that five years earlier had only fifty-nine residents! The new hotel was clearly intended to take care of the future as well as the present needs of the community.

For many years it was managed by Daniel J. Sackman. Sackman had first met Renton when the Captain and his new partner, Daniel Howard, were struggling with the sawmill at Alki. Sackman, then twenty-two years old, helped them move the mill to Port Orchard and became one of the areas first settlers and one of the first loggers for the Renton and Howard mill. In time he became a very successful businessman. He was forty-seven years old when he came to take over the management of the new hotel. Two years later, on November 10, 1877, Sackman married Mrs. Renton's daughter, Elizabeth Sylva Phillips, who had been a widow for eleven years.

Sackman leased the hotel from the mill company and hired others to run it. The first of those was Jack Taylor, a deserter from the English army, whose real name was Jack Halliard.

Staying at the hotel were lumber dealers, salesmen, some ship captains and their families and new immigrants just arrived in Port Blakely. Tourists began coming as the mill grew, and very often the hotel was overflowing, the halls crowded with cots.

There was a saloon in the new hotel and Richard King became its saloon keeper. Port Madison at the north end of the island was "dry", and the saloon at Port Blakely is said to have attracted quite a crowd from there, especially on paydays and weekends.

Besides giving the town class, the new hotel helped to give it form. It was on the north side of the harbor and was east of the mill, the mill company office and store, and the post office, where Renton was postmaster.

Not more than a quarter of a mile across the harbor, south from the hotel and on mill company property, was the community's Indian village. It had been there for some time, long enough to have its own small cemetery. A stream ran down to it through the logged-over hillside. In those days, there was not much else on the harbor's south side, though a few houses had begun to appear on the wide shelf of low-bank waterfront toward the inner end of the harbor from the Indian village. The entire harbor was ringed with low hills whose relatively level tops would soon be farmed.

At the head of the log pond, Renton built four houses for sea captains and their families. While their ships were being loaded in Port Blakely, these esteemed men were housed in comfort in what came to be called the Honeymoon Cottages. The houses were clean and attractive and had the best view of the mill, while being out of the path of its smoke. They were undoubtedly a welcome haven for the captains and their wives, some of whom may have spent a number of weeks at sea. The houses served as an inducement to get captains to do business with Port Blakely rather than another mill town. Today there are linden and locust and other non-native trees growing along the west side of the mill pond, suggesting that some occupants of the Honeymoon Cottages might have brought cuttings from elsewhere, taken them from their shipboard pots and given them a new home at Port Blakely.

The mill company owned and operated a big company store on the wharf near its office and the post office. From it, ships were provisioned and logging camps supplied. All residents of Port Blakely were expected to buy their groceries and household needs there. Nearby farmers naturally made use of the company store. The store carried anything that could be sold at a profit. For the so-called stump ranchers, it even had cattle for sale. As was common in other early and isolated mill towns, the company bookkeeper paid employees by crediting earnings to employee accounts and then charging these accounts for purchases made at the company stores. Residents were captive customers, the store a major profit center for the company.

On September 11, 1876, little more than a year after the formation of Renton, Holmes & Co., the Port Blakely Mill Company was formed as a California corporation to be the operating arm of the organization on Puget Sound. Renton owned 5/12 of its stock, Ham owned 5/12 and Holmes owned 2/12. Six hundred shares of stock were issued and each of these three men gave up one share so three other men could own one share each to qualify as directors. So the ownership was this:

William Renton	249	shares
Richard K. Ham	249	shares
Charles S. Holmes	99	shares
A. L. Taylor	1	share
Walter Sutton	1	share
Thomas Casey	1	share
	600	shares

In December 1876, the partners of Renton, Holmes & Co. turned over all its assets and liabilities in Washington Territory to the new Port Blakely Mill Company. One instrument transferred 3903 acres of timberland. Another transferred all the other Washington assets and liabilities. The documents were filed in Kitsap County on December 18 and 19, 1876. Renton, Holmes & Co. continued as the marketing affiliate in San Francisco.

Lodges of several fraternal orders were established in the community during Port Blakely's early years. The first of these was the Masons, for whom Captain Renton built a hall in 1876. Plans for its construction were announced in this brief news release of February 5: "The Port Blakely Mill Company. is about to begin a hall for the accommodation of religious and other meetings". The lodge was named for Captain Renton, who had become a member of the Masons as a young man. As mentioned earlier, he had sailed to Ireland with food during the famines of the early 1840s. While there he became a member of Union Lodge No. 23 in Newry, County Down. He recognized the value such a lodge would have for his mostly bachelor community at Port Blakely, and thus came into being Renton Lodge No. 29 of the Masons.

Other fraternal organizations followed. Each offered a

more wholesome kind of fellowship than saloons could provide. Prominent among them were Woodmen of the World, the Knights of Pythias, and Evergreen Lodge No. 126, Independent Order of Odd Fellows, more commonly known as the IOOF. They also functioned as protective and insurance organizations. They looked out for their members when they were sick, funded the cost of their most basic needs when they were incapacitated, kept in touch with their home lodges when they couldn't, sometimes offered retirement-home facilities, arranged funerals when necessary, and looked out for widows and orphaned children. In their day, they helped add stability to the new communities of the West.

Unfortunately, the minute books of these organizations stuck very close to lodge business and seldom provided any observations about the larger community. The minutes of the IOOF, which rented space from the Masons, record complaints about the poor lighting in their building, thank the hotel saloon for making cigars available to some of their meetings, and thank the mill company for making one of its tugs available for an outing to visit a neighboring lodge.

Captain Renton's financial success allowed him to be an entrepreneur in other areas during this period. He was the major investor when coal was discovered near Mox LaPush near the south end of Lake Washington—so major, in fact, that the town that grew up there was named Renton in appreciation of his early and substantial support. Frustrated Seattleites, who wanted their city to be the western terminus of a transcontinental railroad, had begun to build their own railroad around the south end of Lake Washington and toward Snoqualmie Pass. Renton was one of the principal financial backers of this effort. In January of 1877, he was one of the thirteen directors elected to the board of this railroad, which they loftily named the Seattle and Walla Walla. The initial portion of the new railroad reached the Renton coal fields.

Lumber shipments from Port Blakely to Honolulu began in the summer of 1878. That port became an important one for the mill company, although the mill at Port Gamble was the first to enter that market and continued to dominate it for many years.

Company ships as well as other domestic and foreign ships often crowded the docks loading lumber, and their crews swelled the population of the little town. One of the mill ships, the 922-ton *Martha Rideout*, had her "day in the sun" when she completed a round trip between Port Blakely and San Francisco in 29 days and 4 hours. This was in 1876 and included the time taken to discharge her cargo in San Francisco. It was a record time, and the ship proudly flew a white flag with a large rooster in the center to commemorate the occasion. Written on the flag were the words "Cock of the Walk." Tacoma Mills, one of Port Blakely's competitors on the Sound, sent the ship's owners a prize broom, which the company was confident it would get back when a Tacoma boat broke the record. But the *Martha Rideout* was so fast, she kept that broom for a good while.

With new and larger passenger steamers serving the coast, starting in 1876, the trip to San Francisco took only six days, even with a stop in Victoria.

More important to most Port Blakely citizens was the twice-daily steamer service to Seattle. The steamer *Success* carried passengers, freight and mail from 1872 until 1885. She was the successor to an earlier service from Seattle to Port Blakely by Colman and Falk. The ease of moving about had certainly improved in the twenty-three years since Captain Renton had first arrived at Alki and later made that Olympia-to-Port Orchard trip in an Indian canoe.

Getting around on land was easier, too. In the summer of 1875, the Bainbridge Hotel established a daily stage between Port Blakely and Port Madison, although one pioneer referred to the road three years later as a "trail." Boats were still the preferred method of transportation.

During these years, the mill was still lighted by dogfish oil lamps, but Captain Renton was working on a plan to illuminate the mill more efficiently. His plan was to extract pitch from sawdust and mix the pitch with oil and grease. Heating the resulting mixture would create a burnable gas. Apparently, there was something wrong with the Captain's bright idea, because the plan was never put into effect.

In the early 1870s, the work force changed somewhat: with the sudden cutback in railroad construction, in which many

Chinese had been employed, the Chinese began to look for employment elsewhere. They were low-cost workers, and a number were hired by the mill. But by 1877, labor strife and anti-Chinese sentiment throughout the region caused the company to give this release to the press: "White men have been substituted for Chinese in the employ of the Port Blakely mill." However, fourteen Chinese were counted in town in the census of 1880.

James Campbell, brother of John and William, came to Port Blakely as a sawmill carpenter in 1879. He was twenty-six and would rise to be another stalwart in the management of the enterprise.

CHAPTER SIX

SOME FURTHER BUSINESS ASPECTS OF RUNNING AN EARLY PUGET SOUND SAWMILL

Lest the passage of nearly 130 years cause one to forget that business is business and that, even in the 1870s, being a successful entrepreneur required paying attention to a myriad of details, some reference to the business aspects of running the Port Blakely Mill Company is necessary. Consider, for example, some of the matters that had to be dealt with during the years 1876 and 1878.

Consider first the log buyer. A sawmill has an insatiable appetite for logs, but the market for its finished product is always changing. One of the challenges facing a mill's log buyer is matching his purchases to the market for the finished product.

Another is buying the right quality and quantity of logs at the right price and having the right inventory of logs at the mill at the right time.

The log buyer at Port Blakely dealt with many loggers at camps up and down the Sound. Here are six extracts from correspondence during the spring and summer of 1876. The reference is always to Douglas fir.

April 29, 1876—Mill to D.J. Sackman (he apparently was still running his logging operation in southern Kitsap and eastern Mason counties as well as leasing the hotel in Port Blakely): Majority of logs in raft must be 32 feet or they will be declined. Tug *Blakely* will bring supplies and pick up raft. (Same message was sent to camps run by Louis Gardner, Follisher & Barrington, and D. Waterman.)

May 18, 1876—Mill to Renton, Holmes & Co. in San Francisco: Piles are very scarce up here so you ought to be getting a better price.

May 24, 1876—Mill to the Adams and Taylor mill in Seabeck: Hear you're about out of logs. If you want some, we have more in our camps up the sound than we want ...We'll tow them around for you.

July 10, 1876—Mill to its field man, M.C. Simmons: You have sent us only three small rafts since November 23, 1875. We cannot see why you employ so many men and put in so few logs. At this rate, it takes more to run the camp than it does the mill! Are you still employing 20 men?

July 29, 1876—Mill to Renton, Holmes & Co.: We have had to throw off some of our old loggers and try new ones to get a better quality of logs.

August 1, 1876—Mill to D.J. Sackman: Can you supply us with a cargo of 350 piles, 65 feet long and 14 inches in diameter? Ask Louis Gardner to help, if necessary.

While there was a sign that the log market might be softening up in the mill's May 24th offer to Adams and Taylor at Seabeck, the correspondence that began two and a half months later suggests that the market for lumber, or at least logs, was definitely in oversupply, and it indicates the variety of ways the company dealt with that reality. It also shows how the pressure to reduce the log production in the camps could be increased and how uncertain long-term employment was in the camps.

August 7, 1876—Mill to its field man, Varner, near Olympia: Get 100 sticks and let us know when you have 30 in the water. Then reduce your force to the lowest possible working gang and cut expenses as low as possible.

August 7, 1876—Mill to its field man, M.C. Simmons: We are overstocked with logs, so reduce your work force and running expenses. But put in all the 24-foot and 32-foot logs you can.

August 10, 1876—Mill to Varner: Hereafter, when you settle with your men, give them drafts on us at 60 days sight (not cashable at full value for 60 days). If they don't like it, let them go.

August 16, 1876—Mill to Varner: Tell Simmons to reduce his work force to 80 men. (Could it have been only 20 on July 10, or was that sarcasm?) We might be obliged to shut the camp down altogether.

August 29, 1876—Mill to Renton, Holmes & Co. in San Francisco: We are closing up the camps as fast as the logs come in. We'll close up all except those furnishing first-class logs.

September 12, 1876—Mill to Varner: We can get all the men we want here, ready and willing to work in the woods for $40 per month. We might try a reduction (in wages) in your camp.

September 16, 1876—Mill to James Long: $5 per 1000 if good as you say.

Extracts from two years later sound a different note.

May 29, 1878—Mill to Varner: Now that you have got into good large timber, cut us a lot of nice ship plank logs.

June 1, 1878—Mill to James Taylor: Please get both of our camps to cut all the 32-foot logs possible.

June 4, 1878—Mill to Amos Broom: Sorry but we're too overloaded with logs to offer to buy yours.

Wonder what was wrong with Broom!

There were many other field men and camp operators in addition to those mentioned above. W.B. Moore was logging for the company at Centerville, G.O. Haller at Coupeville, Elwell at Snohomish, D.O. Pearson at Stanwood, and the firm of Shelton and Forbes at Arcadia, to name but a few of them. Arcadia was in Mason County; the county seat was later named for Forbes' logging partner. The log buyer at Port Blakely had to stay in touch with them all. It's easy to imagine how much pressure he was under and how strained some of his relations with his log suppliers must have been. In 1878, Centerville was moved a short distance and the new community was named

Letterheads, Port Blakely Mill Co. Records, University of Washington, Special Collections.

Stanwood. Stanwood is in Snohomish County near the mouth of the Stillaguamish River.

As observed earlier, San Francisco was the market nerve center for the company. The office in Port Blakely was certainly in daily touch with Holmes and his staff in San Francisco. Here are some market related extracts the mill sent off to Holmes:

> July 3, 1876—Mills at Burrard Inlet (British Columbia) are short of logs. Some ships lying idle there for 60 days. You might take advantage of this.
> September 10, 1876—We have about 1,000,000 feet of logs which we cannot saw to advantage with our present saws—best for flooring.
> September 27, 1876—We sent balance of flat car orders for Canadian Pacific Railway.
> November 25, 1876—We will stop running nights in a fortnight unless anything turns up. A great many camps are shutting down for the winter.
> May 1, 1878—We cut 1,521,000 feet in lumber last month plus 125,000 more used here.
> June 28, 1878—We are able to get logs sometimes for $3.50 or $4.00 per 1,000 feet, but it is impossible to get lumber such as you want for the southern trade out of them. (The 'southern trade' is likely a reference to markets the company had opened on the coasts of Peru, Bolivia, and northern Chile, where the nitrate trade was booming.)

In 1876, the Port Blakely mill was thirteen years old. Its machinery had handled thousands of huge logs. As often as San Francisco could find profitable orders that required it, the mill was run day and night. Maintenance must have required major expenditures of time and money. New and improved equipment was costly, too, but without such expenditures, there was no way that the mill could remain competitive for long. Paying careful attention to plant and equipment was a never ending job.

> September 5, 1876—Mill to Renton, Holmes & Co.: We have to shut down for repairs to back end of mill. It gave way while sawing the big sticks. As soon as we get a good start on Beebee's cargo, we will shut down nights.

Sometimes the correspondence conveyed the sense of delight Renton and the mill foremen must have felt when a new piece of machinery performed in an exceptionally satisfactory manner.

Charles S. Holmes. Photo courtesy his grandson, Stuart Kierulff.

June 21, 1878—Mill to Renton, Holmes & Co.: We have a new gang running and she will do all Prescott represented. Will cut 50,000 feet of planks and boards ...We now want one of Dicey's Patent Edgers—50" type. We want to run eight saws in a set on the gang edger. Yesterday we cut 84,000 feet, chiefly boards with some 6" x 6".

Four extracts from the records of 1876 and 1878 serve as reminders that one of Renton's chief concerns was having an adequate inventory of standing-timber to justify his continued investment in new equipment.

June 20, 1876—Mill to Varner: We send you $500 to pay for 80 acres. On larger purchases we pay $500 to $1,000 down and the balance in a month or so.

August 7, 1876—Mill to Renton, Holmes & Co.: We purchased land last week for $4,000. There is some 15 to 20 million board feet on it, enough to last for several years. We would rather put money into land ...

November 22, 1876—Mill to McNaught and Leary: We have purchased land in Snohomish County for right-of-way.

Sometime in 1878—Mill to A.T. Brown, Registrar at Land Office in Olympia: We enclose land warrant for examination. Please let us know if we can locate 160 acres of land on sound with it.

In 1876, a lot of work was done on the four year old company tug *Blakely*. The correspondence gives the reader the impression that there had been a mishap with her boilers. In any event, it shows another aspect of the business details with which the company office in Port Blakely had to deal.

July 17, 1876—Mill to G.W. Bullene in Seattle: How much will it cost to make patterns for the *Blakely* boilers?

August 2, 1876—Mill to G.W. Bullene: Please send specs on boiler you designed for the *Blakely*. Did you allow for plates up to 5/16 of an inch? They are being shipped from San Francisco.

October 11, 1876—Mill to G.W. Bullene: Foster and Krups bid for making boiler for *Blakely* has been accepted. Have contract drawn for $1,250 and bond them.

It looks as though another problem may have developed two years later.

June 12, 1878—Mill to Renton, Holmes & Co.: Enclosed is a sketch of a shaft to be built for the *Blakely*. Will send coupling from here to be fitted. Also, want a propeller as described. (Description followed)

Many of the communications during this period relate to the purchase of supplies. The purchasing department was charged by Renton with buying at the best possible price, so it dealt with a multitude of competing suppliers located around the Sound and down the West Coast. It is not surprising that the names of most of the well known early merchants on the coast show up in company communications.

Extracts from some letters reveal the ramifications of this aspect of the operation. They also reveal how dependent the mill was on distant suppliers, and they confirm that a grist mill for grinding grain was a normal part of a remote but busy sawmill.

May 11, 1876—Mill to McNaught and Leary in Seattle: We have all the cattle we need, but there are steady inquiries around for them.

May 19, 1876—Mill to Gades: Sorry, we have all the potatoes we can use. Just received 2,013 pounds of sugar from Schwabacher.

June 21, 1876—Mill to Schwabacher & Company: Mike Thielan owes you for a plow. Please debit us and send us bill.

July 20, 1876—Mill to L. Bettman in Olympia: We will order 5,000 pounds of butter at 25 cents per pound.

August 7, 1876—Mill to Renton, Holmes & Co.: Send us three tons of onions (6,000 pounds!) on the return trip of the *Oak Hill* (a company vessel).

August 25, 1876—Mill to Varner: We shall send you the supplies. Does it require such an amount of supplies to run the camp?

August 29, 1876—Mill to Renton, Holmes & Co.: Send us no more grain at present and no more than 200 tons of hay. We do not have so much demand for them at present and will need but little this winter.

August 31, 1876—Mill to Everding & Beebee in Portland: Please send us 1,000 pounds of beans and 1,000 pounds of shoulders. Make prices as low as possible as Seattle prices nearly as low as those in Portland.

September 3, 1876—Mill to W.B. Moore in Centerville: We sent you two tons of good barley today, but no corn, as we don't grind corn except for special orders and had none in stock.

October 28, 1876—Mill to Disston & Sons: Please send following saws to us c/o Renton, Holmes & Co., San Francisco. (A number of different kinds of saws were mentioned.)

December 7, 1876—Mill to Renton, Holmes & Co.: Please send us $3,000 in silver for Christmas. (Silver, like everything else from San Francisco, came north by ship. This order seems to cut the timing pretty close; Christmas was only 18 days off.)

May 14, 1878—Mill to Rothschild Company at Port Townsend: We don't need any Timothy hay at present—getting all our hay from San Francisco.

May 27, 1878—Mill to G.O. Haller at Coupeville: Unless potatoes are coming down about 1-1/2 cents, we don't think you had better send us any more at present.

June 21, 1878—Mill to Corbett and McLeary in Portland: Please send us 1,000 pounds good heavy shoulders, 1,000 pounds bacon, 1,000 pounds dry apples in kegs, 500 pounds oatmeal.

Since the mill dealt with its customers with book credits for earnings and book charges for purchases, it acted in some sense as a bank. In fact, in most cases, it was necessary for the mill to furnish supplies to loggers before the loggers could start cutting the logs for which they would later be paid by the mill. The interest cost of these advances was carried by the company, but the company recovered this cost by reducing the price it paid for the delivered logs. If, for some reason, it was necessary to advance cash, interest was charged at two percent per month.

Drafts were frequently used in the settlement of transactions, and it was often to the mill's advantage to pay for purchases through the issuance of drafts on Renton, Holmes & Co. in San Francisco. Drafts were issued by many firms and the mill office needed to be careful in dealing in drafts of other firms, for frequently they were not worth the amount shown on them. In fact, they might be worth nothing. So, if they were accepted in payment by the mill, they were invariably discounted.

The frontier economy was not a money economy, so the public bodies could seldom pay employees with cash. Instead, they paid by scrip. The mill would discount this scrip, frequently giving only 80 cents worth of merchandise for each dollar's worth of scrip.

For many of its major purchases, the Port Blakely Mill Company needed to use the services of banks. In Seattle, Renton established a good relationship with the Dexter Horton Bank. He borrowed money from Seattle pioneer A.A. Denny. In Olympia, where there were many land transactions, he dealt with the banking house of G.A. Barnes.

The company that Captain Renton founded and that Charles S. Holmes helped him build was successful because the people they employed could deal satisfactorily with each of these details day after day. The details may have varied from year to year, but 1876 and 1878 seem to have been typical.

ह

CHAPTER SEVEN

THEY CAME FROM AFAR—
NILS AND FAUSTA ELOFSON AND
THE SANDERS FROM SWEDEN,
MICHAEL THIELAN FROM
BELGIUM, MERCER GIRL LIZZIE
ORDWAY, AND WASHEE SAM

Early in 1879, the *Tacoma Ledger,* prodding its merchants to get out and hustle for business, made this observation about Port Blakely: "Blakely is the smartest town of its population in these parts and a little trade with it would help New Tacoma immensely".

This "smart" town had indeed taken on the aspects of more than a passing community—and its good reputation spread quickly to all corners of the world. Ships were unloading not only provisions but also the enthusiastic immigrants who gave the community its international flavor.

Nils Elofson was a ropemaker in Norrkoping, Sweden, who had tired of working in a long narrow building, walking backwards weaving strands of hemp together to make rope. He and his wife, Fausta, married just long enough to have a small daughter and another baby on the way, were restless. Like many other residents of Sweden in the early 1870s, they weren't satisfied with the prospects that lay ahead: hard work, low pay and virtually no opportunity to change either.

"America letters," written by Swedish immigrants in America to friends and former neighbors in Sweden, were passed along to Fausta and she shared them with Nils. There was a common thread to them: in America, Canada or the United States, if one were willing to work, there were opportunities.

Among Nils' friends were sailors who brought back stories of the Swedish-like shorelines of Puget Sound, shorelines dense with forests grander than their own. The only inhabited places were on a few harbors where there were docks and tiny sawmills. Perhaps the most important information to get to Sweden, where acquisition of land was so difficult and costly, was that good land was available and inexpensive.

Since emigration would likely mean a lifetime of separation from the families that stayed behind, there must have been doubts about the wisdom of such a move. And there must have been fears about the dangers of the voyage and the frontier. But Nils and Fausta left the Swedish port of Gothenburg on August 6, 1875, giving San Francisco as their destination.

Much has been told about crossing the Atlantic under sail, but Fausta's comment to her granddaughter years later sums it up: "It were terrible", she would say, shaking her head and looking at the floor. The family was sick much of the time, and its quarters on the ship were miserable.

On reaching Port Blakely, Fausta must have been thrilled to be at the end of the journey, no matter the state of the young and rough mill town. And how surprised she must have been to find the practically new Bainbridge Hotel, where her family could bed down for a night or two.

A few other Swedes already lived in the town, so the Elofsons had some help in the new land. In fact, they were soon in what was to be their home for the next four years, a house on the Gus Sanders' farm at Restoration Point.

Sanders was born Eric August Sanders in Sweden in 1848. He emigrated to San Francisco in 1865, where he joined his brother, Charles, in building a schooner. Together they sailed north to Port Orchard. Then Eric moved on to Port Blakely as a "mill builder and sawmill hand". Charles, in 1868, bought Restoration Point as well as the hill and lowland behind it, but soon tired of farming.

He sold the 108.5 acre farm, for which he had paid $200, to his brother, Eric, more commonly known as Gus, for a pair

Gus Sanders farm at Restoration Point. Photo courtesy University of Washington, Special Collections, Dorsaz & Schwerin.

of boots, and Gus took possession of it in 1875, the same year the Elofsons arrived.

Gus Sanders took over his brothers house and soon he and Nils Elofson had built a second home for Nils and his family. They built these and a large dairy barn in the lowland draw close to the shore on the north side of the farm. From their houses the families had an unobstructed view down the Sound. No arriving or departing ships escaped their keen eyes.

The story has been passed down in his family that Sanders would row out with his milk and sell it to the milk-thirsty sailors on board arriving ships as they dumped their rock ballast near Blakely Rocks.

Not long after the Elofsons settled on the Sanders' farm, a second daughter, Sophia, was born. In Sweden, Fausta may have had good help when her first child, Hannah, arrived, but for Sophia's birth, it was quite different; if she had any help it was probably from Mrs. Sanders. There was seldom a doctor in Port Blakely in those early days.

Nils worked at the sawmill at nearby Port Blakely, as well as at Gus Sanders' farm. Jobs on the "green chain", which carried fresh cut lumber to the wharf for sorting and stocking, were easy to come by.

But it was the prospect of owning his own farm that had

drawn him and Fausta to America. Before long he learned that some high and recently logged level land west of the Sanders' farm was for sale. The land was just east of the highest hilltop on the Island. Nils thought it was farmable and took steps to acquire it.

Nils had grown up on a small tenant farm in central Sweden, and the opportunity to own his own land, 160 acres of it, was irresistible. He would be as much an entrepreneur in farming as Renton was in industry.

In 1879, after completing the necessary Homestead Act formalities, the family moved to the level land, calling the hill-top above it Mosebacke after a vista point above Stockholm. The farm was high above the Sanders' farm, which was its nearest neighbor.

To successfully undertake such a commitment, Nils needed tools, his own house, animals, a hired hand. He hauled lumber for the new house up from the mill over what could just barely be called a wagon road. He slowly cleared the stumps, built barns and fences, and planted a large orchard. With Fausta's help he planted a kitchen garden and he needed hay for his dairy cows. It must have been a simple house, but a granddaughter remembers it as wonderful.

Two sons were born while the family lived on the Sanders' farm, and now Fausta had a houseful—four children, with the eldest a mere six years old. Her children soon realized that there was something different about their mother. They could touch her, and even pinch her, and she wouldn't know it. Fausta was handicapped from birth by a partial paralysis on her right side. But her grandchildren remember that she not only washed clothes, but also made them, and that she grew the vegetables she cooked for the family. Her handicap hardly held her back.

The two girls, Mina (as Sophia was called) and Hannah helped their mother in the cool milk room, where the rich cream would slowly rise to the surface of shallow pans of milk. They had a pet raccoon that would get into the milk room if the door was left ajar. One time Fausta found the raccoon, after such an episode, walking down the hill with a great big blanket of cream on his back.

There were goats that helped clear the land, and when they weren't eating underbrush, they were walking on the fence. Years later, Fausta used to giggle when she told her grandchildren about the goats that could walk on the split rails of the fence.

The winter of 1882 was particularly miserable, and little Mina came down with scarlet fever. Her friend, Margaret Sanders, knew that she was sick, and so did Margaret's mother. Mrs. Sanders believed that if her daughter were exposed to Mina's scarlet fever, she would develop an immunity to it, so she let Margaret visit her friend. Soon the dreaded fever was raging in both girls—and both died.

Mina was buried on the farm in a coffin made by her father, with a quiet service over which he presided, reading from the Swedish Bible. Margaret was buried in the Sanders' yard, and a monument marked the spot for years.

Nils had a milk route into Port Blakely; he left early in the morning with his horses Buck and Star, and braked down the steep road (now known as Toe Jam Hill Road) and continued on around the harbor to town. He ladled milk from the cans on his wagon into containers left out by his customers. Fastidious in this as in everything, he had his own high standards of cleanliness, cleaning up a customer's container if it wasn't clean enough to suit him.

Nils expected a lot of his children as one incident shows. A young man named Snap Stewart, tallyman at the mill, was courting the seventeen-year old Hannah. Snap was an adventurer—he'd been cabin boy on several ships by the ripe old age of 15. Nils didn't approve of his advances, but after a whirlwind courtship, Snap ran off with Hannah and married her. This, to say the least, went against her father's grain. Angered by the elopement, and further upset because Snap was Catholic, not Lutheran, Nils disowned Hannah. It was only after the newlyweds had settled in Port Blakely, and a granddaughter, Frances, was born that he relented and accepted the marriage.

Frances Willard Stewart, named for the temperance movement leader of the time, was Nils' and Fausta's first grandchild. She remembers this about the Elofson farm on Mosebacke:

Nils Elofson's farm. Photo courtesy Virginia Elofson Thompson.

My grandfather Nils delivered milk every day. After his route on Saturdays, he stopped in town to pick up our family and drive us up to the farm for the weekend.

Each morning at 5 A.M., Grandma would bring milk and donuts to us while we were still in bed.

Every weekend during the summer she entertained about 20 people for lunch on Sundays; prepared all the food herself. A great variety of food was served in a full course meal; chicken, meat and fish were the staples. All was served on a long table on picnic grounds in the orchard, not far from the house. Also, Grandfather had a keg of beer on hand to serve. After lunch, all the visitors left with fruit and vegetables from the farm.

At milking time, the cats would follow Grandfather to the barn, and they would sit while he squirted warm milk from a cow into their mouths. I would follow Grandmother to the milk house with a spoon under my apron; while she washed pans and milk cans, I would skim the cream off the pans and eat it, but I was never allowed to touch the milk that was to be sold.

For a trick, one of the men at the mill dropped chalk into

a milk can and accused Grandfather of making the milk that way. They had a big laugh, but Grandfather didn't like it a bit.

Years passed, children and grandchildren moved away, and then, after twenty-seven years at Mosebacke, Nils and Fausta sold their homestead, and moved to West Seattle in 1906. They had been willing to work hard and had found opportunity. The orchard that they planted is the only surviving evidence of that hard work, but it still bears fruit and is a poignant reminder of those Swedish pioneers who planted it. The promise of the "America letters" had proved out.

Another immigrant of the 1870s was Michael Thielan, a Belgian. He was one of the many immigrants who brought two cultures together by marrying an Indian. It was only after he and Mary had two daughters that their marriage was "solemnized" in a ceremony at Rolling Bay, probably conducted by the marrying parson, Rev. John F. Damon.

Thielan, who changed his name to Taylor, is best remembered for two things. He acquired the first homestead on the south side of Eagle Harbor. In the 1890s, he sold part of it to the Port Blakely Mill company, and it was platted as the Taylor Addition to Port Blakely. Part of the platted area later became known as New Sweden. The road through it, once called "Lower Road", is now Taylor Avenue. The creek which parallels it is still remembered by some as Taylor Creek.

Thielan is also remembered for the size of his feet. He was a stocky man, and according to pioneer William Grow, boys at the mill used to yell at him, "You would have been a tall man, Mike, if there hadn't been so much of you turned up for feet!".

The Elofson's Swedish and Thielan's Flemish accent soon mingled with accents from Great Britain, Australia, Canada, Chile, China, Portugal, Spain, The Philippines, Japan and France. By the end of the 1870s, the population of Port Blakely was 300, and only one-third of it was born in the United States. Most of the immigrants were from the Scandinavian countries—Sweden, in particular. Most of the men, seventy-six of them, worked in the sawmill, working ten or more hours a day. Others worked in related jobs: there were "surveyors of lumber", blacksmiths, machinists, millwrights, engineers, a saw filer, a bookkeeper and a man who "worked on the logs".

Almost all the mill jobs were dangerous. On the docks, next to the post office, was the fruit, candy and cigar shop of John Showbrook. In Port Blakely, everyone knew the store as "Candy Johnny's". Showbrook, an immigrant from England, was only 37, but he had already been disabled by a circular saw accident. He was fortunate; he survived.

Of course, not everyone worked in the sawmill. Fourteen Chinese still were resident in Port Blakely; Washee Sam, Old John, Old Sam, Loo Yup, Bill Wing, and China Charlie among them. They and their all-bachelor countrymen washed, cooked, waited on tables in the hotel and generally made themselves useful and appreciated. A man from Germany cooked and a man from France was steward at the hotel. Lizzie Ordway, one of the original Mercer Girls and an important figure in Puget Sound educational history, as well as the suffrage movement, was the town's first professional school teacher (1876-1880). She later became the head of Kitsap County schools.

The leading citizens in the mill town, though, were still the Rentons. Captain Renton and his wife, Sarah, lived in the

The Rentons' residence. Port Blakely School on hill. Photo courtesy University of Washington, Special Collections, Watkins 5242.

largest house in town, as befitted a mill owner. The Renton home appears in a photograph taken in 1882 by well-known San Francisco photographer Carleton E. Watkins. It was built well back from Bay Street in the form of a short-legged T, with the foot of the T facing the street. There were three gables, one facing east, one west and a higher one facing the street.

When the house was enlarged, the higher street-facing gable was extended, and a covered porch was put around the new extension. The porch was reached by four steps that came up at an angle to its southwest corner from the entrance path. It seems appropriate that the steps directly faced the mill.

Watkins' photograph shows a barn and a work shed behind the house at the foot of the Port Madison Road hill. A freshly painted and unusually detailed picket fence, complete with newel posts and gate, paralleled the wooden sidewalk along Bay Street. None of the other houses on the street had quite so elaborate a fence.

Judging by the shrubbery next to the house in the Watkins' photograph, the addition was probably finished in about 1878. The addition was needed, because the Rentons were definitely not living alone: they "boarded" Sarah's 40-year-old and thrice-married daughter, Mary Ann Livingston Robinson Gaffney. With her were her four children, ranging in age from twenty-one years to six months.

Close to the Rentons lived their housekeeper, Julia Majors, who also ran a boarding house. Renton, who was sixty-two at the end of the decade and who had become virtually blind by 1874, would "see" his mill through the next decade, but more and more depended on his oldest nephew, John.

ò❧

CHAPTER EIGHT

THE BIG SNOW,
A PRESIDENT VISITS, AND
THE ARRIVAL OF JUDGE PLATE

Nature dramatically opened the 1880s with a pretty January snow. As everyone knows who lives on the shores of Puget Sound, winters are more gray than white, so a winter with some snow is considered by most people, especially children, a welcome novelty. By all accounts, the snow of January 1880 was a record breaker. Seattle pioneer A.A. Denny wrote, "The deepest snow ever known here was in January, 1880, measuring four feet and a half after it had settled and would have measured much more as it fell."

It started on the afternoon of New Year's Day. Shovels and sleds appeared almost simultaneously. The crispness of the air felt good. As the snow began to stick on the limbs of the firs across the harbor and on the spars of ships in the harbor, a scene unfolded familiar to Port Blakely's Scandinavians and New Englanders. The temperature dropped well below freezing, which in the Northwest usually means the air clears and the snow stops falling. That didn't happen this time; the snow continued to fall.

The mill continued to operate, and the longshoremen on the docks continued loading the ships from the untiring green chain that brought the freshly cut lumber to them. At the other

Winter scene at Port Blakely. Photograph by Jessie Kellam.

end of the mill, the men who worked on the logs, getting them from the millpond onto the chains that carried them to the head saw, had to be more careful of their footing. But in their heavy calk boots, foreman George Burchell and his men were able to continue to push the logs around with their pike poles. The logs were huge and hardly bobbed when the men jumped from one to another. That made the job a hazardous one. If a man fell between the logs, he had to struggle to push his head back into the air.

Inside the mill, men were hardly aware that the snow had started. Of course, the man on the head saw knew because part of the log he was sawing had been out of the water and still had snow on it. When he was done with the log, the long cants (big, thick, squared pieces of clear wood) went to the gang saws to be cut into boards. No telltale snow on them.

As people passed each other on Bay Street or on the wharf, the usual remarks made in passing changed to a different kind of talk. Some forecast that the snow would melt by morning.

Others sensed something different about the look of the snow, the way it was falling. They allowed as how, "We might be in for a good one." Of course, with the temperature falling, too, there was the usual concern about frozen pipes. Wooden pipes carried the water from behind the mill company's dam the short distance down to town. Those pipes would probably be all right; but would the smaller ones that went up to each house? They would have to be dealt with. Someone had noticed that ice was beginning to form in a rim around the edges of the millpond. That seldom happened in the mostly saltwater pond.

The steep hill at the start of the dirt road to Port Madison was already becoming impassable, but that wasn't a problem; not many people lived up there, and if someone had to go to Port Madison, such as a salesman or a traveling minister, he would almost invariably go by steamer, going first to Seattle.

Lizzie Ordway, still the only teacher in Port Blakely, and her students met in a small building at the foot of the hill. The mill company donated it and adapted it for school purposes. Since Miss Ordway and her students lived only a short distance from the school, there seemed no possibility that classes would be cancelled, even as the snowfall continued into the evening. She made sure that enough firewood was on hand for the stoves. Just before going home, she got two men going by to sweep the snow off the roof for her. Having grown up in Massachusetts, she knew that accumulated snow could easily crush old buildings. Though plans had already been approved to build a new school near the top of the hill above town, the present one had to do a little longer.

The only person whose job involved moving from place-to-place all day was teamster John Anderson. With his horses and wagon, he delivered supplies to the hotel and the cookhouse. He took newcomers from the steamers to the hotel if they had a lot of belongings and steamer trunks. And there was other moving to be done; more than you would have expected. But no one worried about how John would cope with the snow. He was from Sweden, and this was the kind of winter weather that appealed to him.

There was some worry about the *Success*, the mill company steamer that linked Port Blakely to Seattle. But her skipper, Captain Nugent, knew the course out past Duwamish Head from Seattle, past Blakely Rock and on into Blakely Harbor well. He'd make it fine.

Smoke curled up from the galley stove pipes of the ships at the wharves. Except for one that had finished loading this very day and, therefore, had a full crew on board, most were virtually without crews. Still, it looked like there was someone stoking up the stove fires on each of the ships. The smoke worked its way up through the rigging just as the snow worked its way down to the decks.

It was a pretty scene. The children loved it. By nightfall, enough snow had accumulated so that sledding was possible.

A fire was built in the road at the foot of Port Madison hill. What fun!

Out on the harbor the early dark of winter was broken by only a few lanterns lofted from the rigging of the ships, their yellow light fuzzily penetrating the falling snow.

Jeff Jefferson was the new operator of the saloon at the Bainbridge Hotel and he enjoyed a busier evening than usual. The entrance to the saloon was off the porch at the right, or east, side of the hotel. Inside the hotel, there was good cheer and much conversation with speculation galore about the weather, about ships and how they would manage, about some new equipment in the mill and about construction of a big new shipyard just begun on the harbor. But it was mostly about the weather.

The next morning the forecasters, who had sensed there was "something different" about the way the previous day's snow was falling, were proven correct. People awoke to find that eighteen inches had fallen during the night, and that the snow was still falling hard. As doors were flung open, excited children and their parents could see men walking to work at the mill in perfect quiet; there were no resounding wooden planks underfoot. Their movements were almost ghostlike. Window ledges, porch railings, pointed picket fences, beach logs, everything had its cap of snow. It was a fairyland. There was a new look to everything. Port Blakely could almost have been on a Norwegian fjord or on the rugged coast of Maine. Everyone—well, many people—felt a sense of exhilaration.

Astonishingly, the snow kept falling. When it finally stopped, five feet had accumulated. The early delight changed to real concern. The companys powerful tug *Blakely* arrived in the harbor with a boom of logs in tow from a logging camp run by Asa Fowler. Fowler sent word that it wouldn't be possible to make another boom on schedule if the snow continued. That would soon affect the mills output. So even if the docks were kept clear, there would be no product for the longshoremen to load. Renton and Superintendent John Campbell got in touch with Holmes in San Francisco to inform him of the situation. The telegraph operator reported that he had trouble getting through—the lines were alive with messages.

That day, the mill started up later than usual so that roofs all over town, including those of the mills own buildings, office and store, could be cleared off. As happened all over Puget Sound that year, a number of sheds and flat-roofed buildings did collapse. It was a record snowfall. After it stopped and the weather cleared, the temperature dropped to eight degrees. The snow was on the ground for several weeks. Sadly, depending on one's point of view, the thaw eventually came. The winter, wet again, penetrated everything, and the big snow of January, 1880, became but a memory.

The year 1880 was remembered in Port Blakely because of a Presidential visit made in the fall of the year, as well as because of the major snow storm that began the year. President Rutherford B. Hayes and Mrs. Hayes were guests at Port Blakely on October 12, 1880. As reported in the *Seattle Daily Intelligencer* of October 13, the President and his party arrived on the cutter *Oliver Wolcott*. In the flotilla accompanying them were the *Goliah, Josephine, Libby, Success,* and *Cellelle* on their port and the *Blakely, Fannie Lake,* and *Nellie* on their starboard. The *George E. Starr* was in the center. After the mandatory visit to the mill, where they witnessed a "monster fir log 150 feet long and 20 inches in diameter at the small end—large enough to produce 5,000 board feet of lumber"—as it began its journey through the multitude of saws it would encounter before the last piece of lumber was cut from it. The president then "shook hands all

Mill Company houses. Photo courtesy University of Washington, Special Collections, Watkins 5244.

around" with the townspeople, and then he gave a speech from the hurricane deck of the *Oliver Wolcott*. Then the Presidential party boarded the *George E. Starr* which took them north to visit the mill and town at Port Gamble.

Port Blakely went back to normal and got on with its manufacture of lumber. William Grow recalled, when he was interviewed by the *Bainbridge Review*, that paydays during the 1880s were big events of a different nature. "Every pay night saw the loggers gettin' rid of 30 day's pay in less than that number of hours. Most of the loggers were bad, but not dangerous. After a big drunk on payday, they came back to work happy. With a few exceptions, they were noisy, good natured and generous to a fault."

Grow also remembered that getting about on Bainbridge Island in the early 1880s wasn't so easy. "There were no roads on the island except from Port Blakely to Port Madison. That was an eight-foot dirt track, cut through the woods. There were only a couple of buggies in each of these towns. Dan Sackman, proprietor of the hotel in Port Blakely, kept a livery stable there. At first, when buggies met on the road between the two towns, one of the drivers would have to lift his buggy off the road to let the others pass. Later the commissioners cleared out spots at intervals for passing."

There was some gardening done on the island in those days, but most supplies still came in sailing vessels from San

Francisco; the ships would come in with provisions and return to San Francisco with a load of lumber. Hay was now brought into Port Blakely from the Duwamish and Skagit River valleys, as well as from San Francisco.

Pleasures were simple. Grow recalled, "Everyone went to church, regardless of his weekly activities. Church services were held mostly in the school at first. Parties with dancing were popular, the music furnished by two fiddlers. Young folks as well as our elders knew the steps of the square dance so perfectly that if a caller was not on hand they danced without one."

As Port Blakely became more of a business town early in the 1880s, new services were needed. Charles A. Plate arrived in 1881, shortly to become the town barber and a respected member of the business community. He and his wife, Josephine Jamieson Plate, played important roles in the life of Port Blakely, providing among other things, a touch of culture. He grew up in Wisconsin, the son of an immigrant German musician who at one time had played with a New York City orchestra. She, though handicapped with less than perfect hearing, was a gifted organist, later filling that role in the Port Blakely Presbyterian Church.

Plate came to Port Blakely at the age of 26 to become manager of the hotel for Daniel Sackman, but soon opened the barbershop with which his name was so long associated. Two years after his arrival, he married Josephine in Seattle and brought her, aboard the steamer *Success,* to her new home in the mill town. The extent to which music was a part of their lives is evident by a story told about them: when the Plates were expecting their first child, they went to Seattle to see the opera *Mignon.* Josephine was so thrilled by it that she told her husband she would like to name the baby, if it was a girl, Mignon. He agreed; it was; they did.

The Plates were successful in passing on their appreciation of music to both Mignon and her sister, Jessie. In addition they brought to Port Blakely some of the formality and manners familiar in places more polished than most mill towns. The Plates were generous in taking-in some girls of the immigrant families to teach them "American manners". For a period, Hannah Elofson, Nils and Fausta Elofson's daughter, lived with the Plates, and when she went home on weekends, Fausta would admonish the other children to"do as Johannah does".

The Plate girls did their share of the work around the house and helped their father in his shop. Saturday nights were busy times, with all the shop's chairs filled by loggers wishing shaves as well as haircuts. The girls pitched in to help, and Mignon recalled later that her father "turned his customers out from top to toe". There were two baths and two dressing rooms in the back of the shop, and Charles Plate offered hot baths as well as haircuts and shaves. Mignon and Jessie alternated in keeping the shop clean, and they would take their father his dinner from the house on those busy nights. Their helpfulness in their own family was so evident to mothers in other families that children around town sometimes heard parents say, "If the Plate girls can do it, you can."

The barbershop was right in the middle of town, on Bay Street. Because of its central location, and maybe because barbershops have a way of stimulating conversation, it became an informal meeting spot where men discussed the affairs of the community. The post office was on the wharf just below the barbershop. Johnny Showbrook's candy and cigar store was on the dock, too, and so was the mill company's office and mercantile store. Most all of the business community was at dock level.

In keeping with his efforts to "turn them out top to toe", Charles Plate was not only a barber but also an agent for the Model Electric Laundry in Seattle, which fact he advertised in the Bainbridge Hotel guest register. He was also an agent for the Berlin Dye Works in Seattle, which promised to clean or dye clothes "like new for a nominal sum". Presumably, all over Port Blakely, plumes, furs, gloves, tapestry and rugs were saved from the dust bin by the Dye Works through the efforts of that model of culture and cleanliness, C. A. Plate.

The fact that his peers held Charles Plate in high regard is confirmed by their recommendation of him for the position of Justice of the Peace, a role he held for many years. In fact, he came to be known as Judge Plate, a title that stuck with him the rest of his life.

Judge Plate lived in the mill town for forty-three years,

seeing more change than almost anyone else. He witnessed the boom years of the 1880s and the destruction and rebuilding of the mill in 1888, when it became the "largest sawmill in the world". He saw ships launched from the shipyard, the hotel and school enlarged, the first church built—and its later destruction by fire, two more churches built and families come and go. And he also lived in Port Blakely during its declining years. By the time he and Josephine left Port Blakely in 1924, little remained of what he had seen built.

Josephine outlived her husband and spent her last years living in Seattle with Mignon and her family.

ぎ

CHAPTER NINE

SHIPBUILDERS ISAAC, WINSLOW G., AND HENRY KNOX HALL, AND THE HALL BROS. SHIPBUILDING FIRM

One of Puget Sound's best known shipyards, indeed one of the best known on the Pacific Coast, in the years prior to the turn of the century, was Hall Brothers. It located at Port Blakely in 1880, but before this had been in operation at Port Ludlow, not far inside the entrance to Hood Canal. Isaac and Winslow G. Hall started it when they moved north from jobs at the new U.S. Navy base at Mare Island in San Francisco Bay in 1873.

The Hall Brother's story is so integral to the whole story of Port Blakely that it needs to be told in some detail. It is a story within a story. So if this chapter seems to stray, in terms of detail and geography, and get ahead of the rest of the story in terms of chronology, the reader must understand that it does so only to be fair to the history of the great sawmill's nearest and most important neighbor.

Isaac and Winslow Hall were two of the fifteen children born to George and Cynthia Collier Hall of Cohasset, Massachusetts. Propelled, perhaps, by numbers, six boys in the family sought opportunity on the West Coast. James, the eldest, sailed to California in 1844. He was followed by brothers Isaac, Abraham, Samuel, Winslow G. and Henry Knox Hall.

James continued sailing until he died at sea in 1870.

Abraham engaged in the hay and grain business in San Francisco and built a large house at 1612 Clay Street in 1869. Samuel engaged in the same business in Sacramento, but then moved east to Maine where he went into the lumber business on the Pennobscot River.

Isaac went to work for the Navy's Mare Island shipyard and was later joined there by Winslow. It was from this employment that Isaac and Winslow left to start their own firm at Port Ludlow in 1873. They called it "Hall Bros. Shipbuilding Firm," a title usually shortened to "Hall Brothers." Henry Knox Hall joined them there in 1875.

The shipyard was located beside a sawmill operated by Arthur Phinney. There must have been a number of considerations that entered into their thinking in choosing to locate where the Hall brothers did, but one of them was certainly the ready access to good building materials. Douglas fir was already recognized as a superior material for the construction of wooden vessels. Winter-cut fir was supposed to be the best and have the longest life.

Here is an example of old growth, winter-cut Douglas fir: In 1868, the sidewheel tug *Favorite* was launched at Utsalady on Camano Island. She was acquired by the Port Blakely Mill Company twenty-five years later and used to tow logs and carry passengers for another twenty-five. After she had been in service

The *Favorite*. Photo courtesy University of Washington, Special Collections, UW3911.

a total of fifty years, this was written about her in the Seattle Times on September 11, 1918:

> The *Favorite* is Puget Sounds greatest testimonial to the durability of Washington fir as shipbuilding material. It has not been necessary to renew any of the planking, so far as can be remembered, since the company purchased her. It is as sound and hard today as when the tug sped down the ways at Utsalady. She is regarded as the ultimate test of fir's durability.

The Halls were certainly attracted as well by the length of the timber to which they would have access, a single old growth fir often providing the full keelson of a good size vessel. The wood was easy to work and planks easy to shape to the designer's plan.

During the seven years they operated the shipyard at Port Ludlow, the Halls built thirty-one vessels. The sugar plantations in the Kingdom of Hawaii were undergoing a period of very rapid expansion in the 1870s, and somehow the Halls were able to capitalize on this expansion. Ten of the thirty-one vessels were built for firms in the Islands. Eight of them were two-masted, inter-island schooners of 116 to 140 tons, and two of them were small steamers built for carrying passengers, as well as freight, between the Islands.

Winslow may have been the designer of the Hall Brothers' ships right from the beginning. If not, he soon took on that responsibility. He moved from Port Ludlow back to San Francisco in about 1877, established a company office at 311 East Street on the waterfront, and moved back into his brother Abraham's house on Clay Street. The steamers built at Port Ludlow were towed to San Francisco for their engine installation, and Winslow was in charge of overseeing this activity.

Another reason that Winslow returned to San Francisco, one that will be dealt with more fully later, may have been because the brothers had started to retain a percentage ownership interest in some of the ships they built and may, even during these early days, have done what they did later and built a ship now and then for their own account. They took this vertical integration of their business one step further when they decided to manage their ships and even those of others by finding cargoes, especially for the return voyages of empty lumber ships. San Francisco was the business center for the coast and was the logical place from which to conduct this aspect of the enterprise.

Isaac and Henry remained in charge of construction at Port Ludlow.

Arthur Phinney died in 1877. His affairs became tied up in probate court, and before long his sawmill was closed down. This necessitated the purchase of timbers and planking elsewhere, a costly inconvenience to the firm and a "cause of much delay and vexation" to use the words of Clarence Bagley, writing about the situation in 1916. In 1878, Pope & Talbot bought the mill site, which included the shipyard, determined to expand the mill, and, thus, forced the Halls to look for a new location.

To Captain Renton, it made sense to try to attract the firm to Port Blakely. So he set about trying to persuade Isaac and Henry to make the move. By way of incentive, Captain Renton offered to make land available for the shipyard to the east of the company houses reaching out toward Blakely Point. He also agreed to build a railroad track along the waterfront from the mill to the yard for the movement of timbers and planking. He said he would build the necessary machine shop, and he even agreed to build five houses above the yard, on what became known as Hall's Hill. These were for the Halls and their senior people.

His offer was accepted and in 1879 the decision was made to move. Isaac died that year leaving Henry and his superintendent, George Monk, to accomplish the move.

Naturally there was great excitement in Port Blakely. The shipyard would become a major addition to the town's employment base, boosting it soon by seventy and later by as many as 140 men. New homes, beside the five on Hall's Hill, and new dormitories had to be built. Renton acceded to Daniel Sackman's request that he build an annex to the hotel and to the request of Christian West, the hotel's German cook, that the kitchen facilities be enlarged. Plans were soon approved to build a new and larger elementary school for Miss Ordway near the top of the hill above town and just east of the Port Madison Road.

Construction on the shipyard "ways" began in 1879. Ways are the inclined ramps on which ships are built and sup-

Hall Brothers Shipyard, 1882. Photo courtesy University of Washington, Special Collections, Watkins 5249.

ported during construction. Two double lines of piling, parallel and eleven feet apart, were driven into the sloping gravel beach. Heavy timbers, placed at beach level, reached from each of the piles in one line to their opposite in the parallel line. The piles were aligned so that if a person sighted down them from the upper end, Gus Sander's big white barn on Restoration Point came into view. When the blocks, which held the ship in place on the ways during construction, or later repair, were knocked from under its keel, the ship would slide down backwards, on the greased timbers beneath it, into the water. Soon there were three nearly parallel ways at the site.

The lines of piling reached from well above the high tide line down to below the low tide line. Thus, the ways were over 200 feet long. The ships were built entirely above the high tide line in "stocks" over the upper end of the ways so there was no interruption of work at even the highest tide. To the uninitiated, the ships appeared gingerly balanced on the ways with a high probability that each one would tip over as it slid down the ways into the harbor; but that never happened.

Crowded between the top of the ways and the foot of the bluff, below Hall's Hill, was the loft building, where full-scale plans were spread out so the lines that Winslow Hall designed in San Francisco could be accurately transferred to timbers used in each ships construction. There was a woodworking building, where every timber and every plank was cut to plan size. There was the machine shop. There were sheds for tools, for hardware, for paint and for sails. And there was a shed where oakum was stored. Oakum was a rope-like material impregnated with tar. It was used as caulking between the planks in the hull, as well as the planks in the deck, to make a ship watertight. The smell of oakum combined with the smell of wood shavings and freshly cut wood gave shipyards their characteristic and very pleasing aroma.

The best early description of the shipyard and its product is in the 1881 "Report on the Ship-building Industry of the United States." It was prepared by Henry Hall for Superintendent of the Census, Charles Seaton. Hall signed his report as "special agent." He was no relation to the Hall brothers of the shipyard. The report starts out by stating there were eleven shipyards in the Washington Territory in 1881; all of them on Puget Sound. About Port Blakely, Henry Hall wrote:

> The owners have fitted up the Port Blakely yard at considerable expense and have sent a delegate to Bath, Maine, to report on labor-saving appliances there employed and to purchase steam saws, planers and a full line of equipment for their yard. Their schooners are fast, handsome and popular, and have long, sharp bows, with slightly hollow lines, the top sides having a faint curve home, and at the stern round in sharply over the arch-board in a strikingly graceful fashion. There is not a straight line on the surface of the hulls anywhere ...the average length of stuff (the planking) is 20 feet longer than that of eastern yards... Located near a large sawmill, the Halls have run a light railroad track down to the mill and bring up their lumber on platform cars. Nearness to the mill enables the builder to order timber as fast as he needs it and to save the cost of transportation... A barkentine 180 feet in length, 162-1/2 feet on the keel, 38 foot beam and 15 feet hold was in frame at the time. The keel was in two pieces, one of them 126 feet long and 26 inches deep by 15 inches wide. The frames

(ribs) were 22 inches by 16 inches. The planking was five inches thick and the decking four inches thick.

The agent writing the report was speaking of the ship to be christened the *Makah*, launched in 1882. First ship to be launched that year, the *Makah*, at 700 tons, was the largest by a wide margin, of anything the yard built during its first eight years at Port Blakely.

Although his report was focused on shipbuilding, agent Henry Hall incorporated in it some more general observations about the appearance of Puget Sound and Seattle at the time of which he wrote:

> Fir forests completely cover the face of the land to the water's edge, and the view from the steamboats is (of) an unbroken wilderness of dark green trees as far as the eye can reach, with towering snow-clad mountains rising here and there from its surface... The first steam mill on the Sound was set up at Seattle in 1853, and although it has been in operation for 30 years, the only observable impression that has been made on the dense fir forests is the clearing of a space for the town to stand on. The town is a large collection of houses, spreading all over the side of a hill which rises at the head of a deep bay, and stumps of trees are scattered all through.

The earliest photographs of shipping at Port Blakely show square-rigged sailing ships almost exclusively. Such ships were well suited for long voyages, voyages in the nitrate trade that took them to Peru, Bolivia and Chile and then around Cape Horn to Europe. Nitrates were the chief export and sustainer of the economies of those three South American countries. They were used principally in the manufacture of fertilizer and explosives. Handling all the sails and rigging of these ships required large crews, and they were relatively poor performers when the wind was not from nearly straight behind them. Furthermore, they required a substantial amount of ballast when sailing empty. For the short trip to San Francisco from Puget Sound and return, a ship was needed that could sail well in both directions, sometimes with the wind and sometimes against it. And the smaller

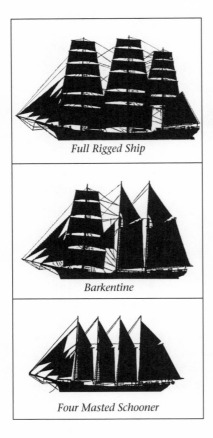

Full Rigged Ship

Barkentine

Four Masted Schooner

the crew required, the better. Barks and barkentines, which used gaff-rigged or fore-and-aft sails on one or two of the aft masts of a three-masted sailing ship were a partial answer. A large schooner would prove the best answer.

Winslow Hall was largely responsible for the design of the lumber schooner that carried only fore-and-aft sails and sometimes was outfitted with topsails above them. Such a ship required a significantly smaller crew than the old square-riggers, barks and barkentines. The crews were reduced further still with the advent of the steam donkey engine in the early 1880s. It aided immensely in hoisting the sails, raising anchors and in working the bilge pumps. The Hall-designed lumber schooner had the additional advantage of requiring little or no ballast.

John Lyman, in his article, *Sailing Vessels of the Pacific Coast, 1850–1905*, described Winslow Hall's ships in this way:

> By giving the ends of the hulls plenty of fineness and a fair amount of deadrise to the floor, enough immersion was secured to enable the vessel to sail empty without ballast. Baldheaded schooners were a favorite berth among sailors in the coasting trade, as in the long beat to windward on the return trip there were no gaff-top-sails to shift when tacking.
>
> Newcomers to the trade were amazed at the way a lofty barkentine (or a schooner) could stand up empty with only a

few tons to put her in proper sailing trim. Sheer was reduced to a minimum to enable long timbers to be stowed on deck; and since lumber is not harmed but actually improved when carried on deck, a vessel frequently was designed to carry over half her cargo this way.

To this end, even the largest of the fleet was built with but a single laid deck and not more than a few beams in the hold. Longitudinal strength lost in this way was gained back by increasing the keelson and thickening the ceiling planking out to the turn of the bilge... In lumber capacity the West Coast vessel could carry 130% of her net tonnage, while her steel competitors stowed just under 100% and Down East wooden square-riggers with their three decks and appurtenant knees could not lift over 80% and required ballast underneath in addition.

What a keen analyst of a ships performance Winslow was and what an innovator of new design. Mr. Lyman's article, though covering all the builders on the coast, seems to highlight the Hall Brothers' ships. Only in one particular does he mention a shortcoming. Even this one must have been preferred by crews to climbing aloft in square-riggers.

...when heavy perishable cargo such as sugar or nitrate had of necessity to be stowed all below deck, the West Coast lumber vessel rolled at her miserable worst.

The first vessel built by Hall Brothers at Port Blakely was the 365-ton three-masted schooner *Maria Smith*, launched June 4, 1881. While the firm built a bark and five barkentines during the first seven years after the move to Port Blakely, it also built fifteen three-masted schooners. One was the 447-ton *William Renton*, launched soon after the *Makah* in 1882.

Today it is easy to think of these sailing ships as romantic symbols of a bygone era and to forget the business realities they represented. They were, of course, essential for marketing the output of all the pre-railroad cargo sawmills. Ideally, the mill owner preferred that ships owned by some other party carry his lumber. He preferred to be spared the cost of owning a fleet. Such ownership simply diverted his limited funds from modernization and expansion of his mill or, later, from the purchase of timberlands. But there were also reasons why he didn't like to be solely dependent on ships owned by others. Whenever the demand for lumber was strong, so was the demand for ships, and then rates skyrocketed and availability diminished. This resulted in poor service to customers as well as high transportation costs. So the major mill companies usually owned at least a few ships of their own.

This was not without problems. Although a full cargo could be virtually guaranteed on the outward-bound voyage, the mill owner had no such guarantee of a cargo on the return voyage. In fact, for voyages to any port other than San Francisco, there was seldom any cargo moving from the lumber-using destination back to the lumber-producing point of origin. The best that could usually be hoped for was to pick up a cargo that was headed in the general direction of the sawmill. To have a ship return from Australia or South America in ballast, without cargo, was costly indeed.

Renton and the Hall Brothers came to a joint ownership agreement that benefitted both companies. The financial strength of Renton's mill was never in doubt, so the Halls would

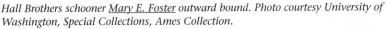

Hall Brothers schooner <u>Mary E. Foster</u> outward bound. Photo courtesy University of Washington, Special Collections, Ames Collection.

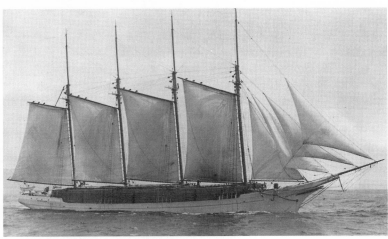

often retain an interest in the ships that were sold to the Port Blakely Mill Company. These jointly owned ships were managed in San Francisco by Winslow Hall who then shouldered the responsibility for finding return cargoes. One of the lumber-using destinations that usually offered a good return cargo was the Kingdom of Hawaii.

The relationship that the Hall Brothers' shipyard had established with growers and shippers of sugar in Hawaii, while the yard was located at Port Ludlow, continued after the move to Port Blakely. The only serious competition seems to have come from the builder Mathew Turner in San Francisco, and there apparently was enough Hawaiian business for both yards.

A good customer in the islands was Foster and Company which operated Inter-Island Steam Navigation Company. Several steamships were built for the company after the move to Port Blakely; the first one being the *James G. Blaine.*

Launched in 1884, the *James G. Blaine* was the largest steamer thus far built on the Sound. In *Hawaiian Interisland Vessels and Hawaiian Registered Vessels*, author Mifflin Thomas gives this information about her:

> Wood screw steamer, 500 gross tons, 380 net tons, 158.1' x 30.5' x 12.7'. Built at Port Blakely in 1884 by Hall Brothers for the Inter-Island Steam Navigation Company. Two cylinder compound engines, 20" and 40" diameter cylinders with 30" stroke by Hinckley, Spiers and Company of San Francisco. Three furnace Scotch boiler, 12 feet diameter and 10 feet 6 inches long. 73 net horsepower, speed 10 knots. Named *James G. Blaine* on launching, but on arrival in Honolulu October 27, 1884, renamed *W.G. Hall.* Very similar in appearance to the *Mikahala,* built later the same year by Hall Brothers for the same firm. Cost $45,000. Accommodations for 36 cabin and 119 deck passengers. Could haul 6,000 bags of sugar.

Successful as these steamers were, the market for them was limited. So the lumber schooner remained Hall Brothers' most familiar product. Captain Renton was pleased with the performance of the schooners built for the mill company, but he and other mill owners wanted larger ships. So Henry Hall asked

Winslow to send the designs for a four-masted schooner. Hull No. 57, the 26th hull laid at Port Blakely, was the first of a successful series of four-masted schooners. The finished vessel was christened the *E.K. Wood* when she was launched in 1888 for the E.K. Wood Lumber Company of Hoquiam, Washington. This was a ship of 521 tons, compared to the largest three-masteds 480 tons and a more normal three-masted tonnage of 430. The *E.K. Wood* met the mill owner's wish for greater lumber-carrying capacity, sacrificed nothing in speed and needed no greater crew than the smaller ships. Winslow Hall had designed another superb ship, and the four-masted schooner became the yard's stock-in-trade for as long as the firm operated at Port Blakely.

Three ships were launched in 1889. One was the four-masted schooner, *Robert H. Lewers*, built for Lewers and Cooke to replace the *Hope*, which burned that year on her way to San Francisco. Lewers & Cooke was a major lumber dealer in Hawaii, and its ships carried lumber from Puget Sound to the Islands and sugar from the Islands to San Francisco. The other two were the *Golden Shore* and the *Irmgard*.

The census for 1889, the year of statehood for Washington, records that seventy men were employed at the Hall Brothers yard. Among them were familiar names. One was Henry Knox Hall, age fifty-eight. Another was his son, James W. Hall, age twenty-five, who was shown to be a ship's carpenter. Edward Hall Lincoln was listed as timekeeper. Also listed as working at the shipyard was William Campbell, age sixty-one. William was Renton's brother-in-law from Nova Scotia. Margaret Renton Campbell, his wife, was listed in the census, too.

In 1891, Hall Brothers launched a sister ship to the *Robert H. Lewers*, the 732-ton schooner, *Alice Cooke*. She, too, was built for the firm of Lewers and Cooke. Both vessels had long careers.

The *Alice Cooke* was named for the three-year old daughter of C.M. Cooke, a partner in the firm. She was first commanded by Captain D.P. Penhallow, who became one of the longest serving sailing ship captains in the West Coast lumber trade. His ship gave a good account of herself. She traded steadily for the next thirty-four years between Hawaii and the West Coast; all of those years under the Lewers and Cooke flag.

Each ship launched from the yard added to the firm's reputation as a builder of ships of high quality and performance. By 1894, fifteen four-masted schooners had been built. Winslow Hall, who had moved to an office at 28 California Street in San Francisco, now proposed to build a five-masted, 900-ton schooner. In May, 1896, Hall Brothers laid the keel of the *Inca*, the first five-masted schooner to be built on the West Coast. In November, the big ship was ready for launching. For such a major event, the Port Blakely schools were closed so students could participate. One of them, nine-year-old Melusina Thornton, daughter of Chief Engineer Thornton of the steamer *Sarah M. Renton*, christened the *Inca*. The ship was 215.5 feet long, 41.3 feet wide and 16.5 feet deep and could still be operated with a crew of eleven.

Flying from the mast of the *Inca*, when she slid down the ways, was the Hall Brothers' house flag, a tapering swallow-tailed banner, half blue and half red, with a large white "H" in its center.

Today the Columbia River Maritime Museum of Astoria, Oregon owns a fine model of the *Inca*. Not long ago, they published these lines about her:

> The *Inca* was a particularly handsome vessel, and she was well kept. She was a superb example of the West Coast lumber carrier, and the first orthodox five master built on the West Coast. She was typical of her class, from the fine lines of her clipper bow to the ringtail topsail carried over leg-o-mutton spanker. She spent most of her time in offshore trade, principally carrying lumber in her holds and in huge deckloads, to New Zealand and Australia.

Other ships launched during the 1890s carried such now familiar names as *W.H. Talbot, Lyman D. Foster, C.S. Holmes, John A. Campbell, Annie M. Campbell, Mary E. Foster,* and *Winslow*.

The *Winslow* was launched in 1899 and named in memory of Winslow G. Hall who had died the previous year at age 65. A maritime career of note had come to an end. Winslow Hall had carried a big load in San Francisco. He had lived modestly and always at 1612 Clay Street with his brother Abraham. He was buried at Cypress Lawn Cemetery in San Francisco. A number of years later, Henry Knox Hall was buried in the adjacent plot.

The *Winslow* and the other ships just named were all four masted schooners. By the end of the century the yard at Port Blakely had launched twenty-seven of these superb sailers. To start the new century, they launched another, the *Bainbridge*, and ten more followed her. Some of them sailed for many years; together, they were an appropriate memorial to the man who designed them and to the company that built them, too.

The Hall Brothers' ships were designed not only to sail well but they were designed with the comfort of the crew, at least the officers, in mind. The *James Tuft* was a four-masted barkentine launched from the shipyard in Port Blakely in 1901. She was 215 feet long with a maximum width of 42 feet. The quite spacious living quarters for the captain and his officers were under the poop deck at the stern or after end of the vessel. For many years, from her launching until about 1922, these quarters were occupied by Captain August Fridberg and often by his family. The captain's wife was Elenora Elofson, Port Blakely shoemaker Elof Elofson's daughter and niece of dairy farmer Nils Elofson. She and her two children lived on board until 1912, when it was time for the oldest child, Anna, age 8, to go to school ashore. Anna and her brother, young Gus, remembered those years at sea vividly.

Gus lived in an alcove off his parent's room and his clothes were kept in a drawer below his built-in bunk. Anna recalls that the built-in bunks were preceded by iron beds that were anchored to the floor. Elenora taught her children the three R's, read to them, and did her sewing in the master's study. This cabin also contained the master's desk and a number of storage drawers for clothes, but the children called it "Mother's room." The other rooms—the master's bedroom and the dining room—were quite spacious.

The mates and the ship's carpenter lived in the after end of the ship, too. There was an entrance for the master and his family and another for the mates. This second entrance led to the dining room, where the master, his family, the mates and the ship's carpenter had their meals. Off the dining room, on the port side, was the pantry. Food was prepared in the main galley and brought to the pantry at meal times. At the forward end of the master's quarters was a cargo lazarette. A water closet and washrooms completed the quarters. Port holes let daylight into every room.

Anna and Gus remembered that about a dozen chickens were kept on deck to provide fresh eggs and, toward the end of the journey, fresh chicken for the family. The sailors caught flying fish, which the cook prepared into a delicious dish.

1901 saw the launching of Hall Brothers' Hull No. 100, the 626-ton *Gamble,* for Port Blakely's big competitor up on Hood Canal. The same year saw the launching of the four-masted schooner *Alpena.* She was made famous in 1909 by a near disaster and a heroic recovery at Newcastle, Australia, when she was under command of Captain A. Neilsen. She carried a load of timber for the coal mines near Newcastle. The huge 1,237-ton five-masted schooner, *H.K. Hall,* launched in 1902, was followed by the *Blakely,* a four-masted schooner. It was high time some-

Loading the schooner Blakely. *Photo courtesy Puget Sound Maritime Historical Society, Williamson Collection.*

one christened a ship after the name of the harbor on which the yard and the sawmill were located. The *Blakely* was typical of most of the four-masted lumber schooners built by Hall Brothers—751 tons and 900,000 board feet capacity.

The captain's quarters on the *Blakely* may have surpassed those of the *James Tuft*. Hard as it is to believe, chairs in Queen Anne or 17th century style, a five-drawer bureau, wall mirrors, a piano, a traditional iron bed and oriental rugs were among the furnishings. In one photograph of the ships interior, the only thing that looked like it might safely ride out a storm at sea was a bird cage hanging from a ceiling hook. Nothing else looked "anchored down." Sun, diffused by pretty polka dotted Swiss curtains, poured into the room through two square windows, not portholes. It highlighted the detail of the gleaming wood-work and reflected from the high gloss of the freshly painted panels of the door and the walls. The oriental rug looked made for the room—it's hard to think of it as a cabin—and reached wall-to-wall. As if to add an extra touch of luxury, a tasseled oriental throw rug lay between the captain's bed and the bureau. Pictures, books, pillows, doilies, a piano stool and music on the piano, and a hanging kerosene light added to the civilized look of the quarters.

Was it possible that the *Blakely* went to sea like this? Almost certainly not. But like other commodity and bulk-carrier sailing ships of the day, she was sometimes in port longer than she was at sea. That was especially true in the coastal lumber trade, where loading and unloading usually took longer than the round-trip voyage. There was every reason for the cabins to look like rooms at home during those periods. At sea, the rooms would have looked like the cabins they really were; the furniture lashed down and probably out of sight, replaced by a navigator's table complete with instruments, Bowditch tables, charts and log books.

In many ways, the people who worked at the shipyard were a large and happy family. There were frequent excuses for a party, since there were three or four ship launchings most years. Flags and flowers made the launchings festive, and everyone in town flocked down to the dock for the fun. The Hall Brothers' house flag—that tapering swallow-tailed banner, half blue and

The interior of the 4 masted schooner <u>Blakely</u>, built at Hall Brothers Shipyard in Port Blakely as Hull Number 106 and launched in 1902. Note the detailing in the woodwork and the fine furnishings! Photo courtesy San Francisco Maritime Museum.

half red, with the large white "H" in the center—always flew for the occasion.

Although everyone knew the Hall brothers, they were not the only individuals whose roles were vital to the success of the shipyard. At Port Blakely, George Monk played one of those vital roles; George E. Billings played another from his San Francisco office.

Monk, who ran the shipyard as superintendent for the Halls, had come to Port Blakely from Plymouth, England, via Australia and Port Ludlow. He started work for the Halls at Port Ludlow at the age of twenty-eight in 1873 and stayed with the company twenty-seven years.

By 1892, everyone in the mill town considered Monk to be a confirmed bachelor. He had lived alone in one of the smaller houses up on Hall's Hill above the shipyard for twelve years. As it turned out, he had just never met the right girl. He met her that year in a way he never could have anticipated.

Anna Saunders grew up in Plymouth, England, many years after Monk had left. She and her brother emigrated to Victoria, British Columbia, where Anna was engaged to be married; but her fiance left her waiting at the altar. Instead of returning to Plymouth, Anna and her brother wrote home that they were staying in Victoria. Some mutual friends of the Saunders and George Monk, never giving up hope on George, wrote him from Plymouth about this attractive girl and her plight. He took the cue, went to Victoria, courted Anna, married her in February of 1893 and brought her to Port Blakely.

Seven years later, in 1900, George received an offer he couldn't refuse—to become a shipbuilding foreman for the big Moran Brothers Shipyard in Seattle. He accepted the offer and moved on. He was 55 years old and had spent half of his life with Hall Brothers, where he played a key role in building sixty-two ships at Port Blakely, as well as thirty-one at Port Ludlow.

George and Anna Monk's son, Edwin G. Monk, made just as fine a name for himself as a Seattle-based designer of power boats as his father made as Superintendent of Hall Brothers.

As observed earlier, from the day the Halls decided to retain a full or partial interest in some of the ships they built, there was the problem of how to schedule them efficiently. Abraham and Winslow looked after this during the company's first years. George E. Billings who married into the Hall family in San Francisco was their successor. He was thirty-four when he married Abraham Hall's daughter Susanna Maria in 1885. He was in the book-selling and stationery business, but when he met Winslow Hall, he decided the shipping world was more interesting. He persuaded the Hall brothers to take him on as bookkeeper and he worked for Winslow Hall for ten years in this and other capacities. Then, in 1895, his mentor for those years, recommended that Billings be named manager of the firm in San Francisco.

In the words of Robert E. Ficken, in his 1987 book *The Forested Land*, "Prior to the completion of transcontinental railroads to Puget Sound, the economic well-being of western Washington was more closely linked to that of Honolulu, Callao,

Sydney, and Melbourne—more closely related to Hawaiian sugar and Latin American and Australian minerals—than to developments in the domestic American economy east of the Cascades. Northwest lumbermen were among the leading traders in the international emporium that was the Pacific Ocean." Billings was a major participant in that emporium.

The responsibility for finding cargoes and scheduling the Hall Brothers' fleet and other ships in which the company had an interest now rested with Billings. He kept in touch with markets and shippers all over the Pacific Ocean.

There was a myriad of details connected with these responsibilities. The most important one was finding good captains. They were the ones who oversaw the loading and unloading of cargoes, who could prevent port delays leading to costly demurrage charges and late deliveries to customers. In their hands were the decisions about repairing ships, if necessary, away from home port. Ultimately, all these matters came back to headquarters and had to be dealt with there as well. Billings delighted in this work and earned the honor of having a ship named for him.

Port Blakely's third five-masted schooner, built in 1903, was christened *George E. Billings*. She was as large as the first two five-masters, registering 1,260 tons. These ships must have been a challenge to build in the always tight shipyard quarters at Port Blakely. The *Billings* could carry 1,500,000 board feet of lumber, a full week's output of the mill there. Most of her ocean passages were faster than average. Her final voyage under sail was made "in ballast" more than twenty years after her launching, a disappointing, unproductive way to end a profitable career. A fishing barge after 1926, the aging *Billings* was towed to sea and burned off the California coast in 1941.

The man, for whom this final of the five-masters was named, cared about sailing as a pastime as much as he cared about ships and shipping as a profession. Recognizing Billing's love of sailing, his friends and fellow members elected him the third Commodore of the Corinthian Yacht Club at Tiberon in Marin County, across the bay north of San Francisco. Not far away, in Mill Valley, he built a beautiful home beside a redwood shaded stream. He called it Redwood Lodge. Even today it reflects the prosperity of the period in which it was built; a prosperity that for many in San Francisco grew out of their business ties with Puget Sound shipbuilding and lumber firms.

Returning to Port Blakely, it is appropriate to say a few words about the shipyard's timekeeper of 1889, Edward Hall Lincoln. In 1885, he arrived in Port Blakely as a twenty-two-year old in search of a job. He stood a better chance than some because his mother, Anne Jane Hall Lincoln, was one of Henry Knox Hall's sisters. But there was more reason than that to hire him. Edward had experience in shipbuilding in Cohasset, Massachusetts. He came to Port Blakely well recommended and was put right to work in the yard. But the fall of 1885 was so wet and miserable that he told his uncles he couldn't stand it. He returned to Cohasset, endured a cold, snowy winter there, decided rain wasn't so bad and returned to Port Blakely. Lincoln started at the shipyard as a bandsaw operator, became the time-keeper and later was the bookkeeper.

Edward Hall Lincoln married Jennie Elofson, sister of Captain Fridberg's wife, Elenora, and daughter of Elof Elofson, the shoemaker. For her he built a large house near the beach, just beyond the shipyard, on the path out to Blakely Point. Almost 100 years later, it is still standing and recognizable as the home that Lincoln built.

Edward Hall Lincoln's younger brother, Charles James Lincoln, was born in 1878 at Taunton, Massachusetts. He came to Port Blakely at age seventeen and is remembered as a pho-tographer who left dozens of glass plate negatives from which some of the finest pictures of the shipyard, mill, town, and harbor have been produced. The photographs give an excel-lent understanding of the appearance of the mill, the ships in the harbor, and especially of the activity at the shipyard during the years 1895 to 1905.

This story within a story about shipbuilders Isaac, Winslow and Henry Knox Hall is not quite complete, but it is appropriate now, to return to Puget Sound of the 1880s and pick up the story of Captain Renton and his sawmill.

CHAPTER TEN

SOL SIMPSON AND THE BLAKELY LINE

Anewspaper article in 1882 described Renton, Holmes & Co. in this way: "The company has a great mill at Port Blakely, seven sailing vessels and a steam tug. The mill has been enlarged and is 490 feet long and 90 feet wide. The power is steam. It cuts logs that are 6 feet in diameter and 145 feet long. There are numerous electric lights, so that on the short winter days there shall be no darkness to obstruct the manufacture and shipment of lumber during working hours. In 1881, seventy vessels took cargoes of lumber from the mill." Envious Seattleites are said to have wondered how a mill town like Port Blakely could have electric lights when a "city" like Seattle didn't.

The mill at Port Blakely in 1882 was said to have a capacity of 200,000 board feet a day, the greatest capacity of any sawmill on the Pacific Coast. While small by later standards, that still was a lot of wood. It meant the mill could produce each day almost 38 miles of planks 12 inches wide and 1 inch thick. At the time, the mill at Port Gamble had a capacity of about 175,000 board feet a day, and the one being built at Port Ludlow would match Port Blakely's capacity. These three were said to be the largest capacity mills on the Coast. To keep them supplied with logs was a major endeavor.

It was clear to Captain Renton and his two San Francisco associates, Richard Ham and Charles Holmes, that their mill's future depended on a reliable, long-term source of timber, one that the mill company controlled. It wouldn't even make sense to make improvements in the mill itself unless timber enough for years of operation could be secured. As the sawmill at Port Blakely approached its twentieth year, logs were coming to it from thirty-two different logging camps. Much of the timber within easy reach of the mill had been cut, pulled to the beach, made into booms and towed to Port Blakely or some other mill town. So Renton had scouts searching for timber back some distance from the waters of Puget Sound.

The owners of Puget Mill Company, later Pope & Talbot, who built their sawmill at Port Gamble, also recognized the need for a long-term timber source and did something about it early on. But it was the only firm that had the financial resources to buy land, and its owners were perhaps the only operators whose previous experience made crystal clear the necessity of buying it. They were from the lumbering and shipbuilding town of East Machias, Maine, where their families had owned and operated sawmills and seen their timber resources depleted to such an extent that shipbuilding timbers were now often sent there from Puget Sound. In 1861, when the opportunity occurred to buy University of Washington land-grant land, Puget Mill Company acquired over 15,000 acres of it, right around the mill at Port Gamble, for $1.50 an acre. By 1864, the company owned more than 32,000 acres, and with those wise early purchases, the company established a base that enabled it to continue in operation until September 30, 1995.

Following that example, Renton's scouts were no longer looking for small tracts of timber. It was too expensive to establish a camp and build roads that could be used for only a short time. What was needed was acreage that would justify both a more permanent base and a transportation system that could improve on long hauls over dogfish-oiled skid roads. Not the first one to have the idea but a pioneer in implementing it, Captain Renton had in mind building a railroad into the timber. He would then use skid roads—roads made of heavy timbers over which logs were dragged by horse or oxen—as feeder roads, not main lines.

Renton picked on Mason County as his primary source of timber. He hired John B. Forbes as his agent to cruise the timberlands, select acreage and secure title to controlling pieces of it. Forbes worked unceasingly and as quietly as he could. By the end of 1882, he had acquired 22,000 acres and had obtained the right of way to build a railroad from Little Skookum Bay into the timber.

Railroads had already been used in the woods, but not extensively. Renton knew something of their value as bulk carriers from their use in carrying coal. C.H. Hanford wrote of this latter fact in his book, *Seattle and Environs*, when he said this about Seattleites' efforts to build a railroad east, the Seattle and Walla Walla Railroad, starting in May, 1874:

> The right-of-way was cleared and the roadbed levelled for about three miles. Next, a piece of road (a narrow gauge railroad) was built and put into operation extending from the coal mines at Renton (not so named until many years after 1874) to a steam boat landing on the Duwamish River for hauling coal from the mines. That much was accomplished with money furnished by William Renton, principal owner of the Port Blakely sawmill and W.H. Talbot of San Francisco, who were interested in the coal mines.

Sophie Frye Bass, in her story, *When Seattle Was A Village*, says this about Renton's early railway experience:

> By the last of April, 1877, the Seattle and Walla Walla had been formally opened to traffic. At this time, Captain William Renton took over the management of the coal mine. It was not until after Captain Renton began to develop the mine and after the railroad was completed that the output of coal really began.

His building a railroad into Mason County timber would draw on this experience.

The *Puget Sound Weekly Courier* of Olympia carried this story on December 15, 1882:

> An enterprise will soon be inaugurated by Captain William Renton of the Port Blakely Mill Co., and that is the building of

a standard gauge railroad from the head of Little Skookum Bay toward, and eventually to, Elma on the Chehalis River. He has secured one of the most valuable bodies of timberland in Western Washington. The railroad will run most of its way through this timber, about 1,000 million feet of it. Right-of-way and terminal facilities have already been secured. From 250 to 400 men will have constant employment in the camps and with the railroad.

This was an enormous undertaking in every way. Holmes and Renton exchanged many letters on the financing of the venture.

The name of the line was to be the Puget Sound and Grays Harbor Railroad, but it was commonly called The Blakely or The Blakely Line. The terminus of the logging railroad, where logs could be dumped into saltwater for towing to Port Blakely, was near Kamilche, and it was located at the entrance to Little Skookum Bay, seven miles south of what became the town of Shelton. Work on the railroad started in the spring of 1883. Not much progress seems to have been made until three years later when Renton hired Sol G. Simpson to grade the line for the railroad. Simpson had come to Seattle from Nevada in 1877, and developed a successful contracting firm that "graded" new streets in the city. His arrival was too late for him to have worked on the original section of the Seattle and Walla Walla Railroad; but he may have gained some railroad experience on the extensions to Black Diamond and Franklin.

According to Robert Ficken's *Lumber and Politics*, Sol Simpson arrived at Kamilche with "a crew of experienced road builders and a few horses. A forceful and innovative man, the wiry Simpson quickly impressed his new associates." A Port Blakely Mill Company official found him "a pleasant man, easy to get along with . . . a man who is conscientiously honest."

On May 2, 1888, chief engineer H. Tilly Brown wrote to Port Blakely that the fourth mile of track was finished. Grading of miles five and six would, Brown thought, cost about $4,000 per mile. He said that 100 men and four carts were being used and that the number could be doubled if necessary. Simpson was using horses in place of oxen as they were more efficient. By this year, The Blakely was hauling out an average of 225,000 board feet of

Men taking a break from laying railroad track into the forest.

logs a day—a 150-percent increase over 1886 production.

Mason County timber was by far the mill's largest source, land holdings in the county having grown to 80,000 acres by 1887. Simpson was doing a fine job of getting it out, as well as pushing the railroad on into the virgin stand. Perhaps in an effort to keep him challenged and with the company, Renton promoted Simpson. In 1889, he became superintendent of all operations of The Blakely Line. Simpson, however, was already on his way as an entrepreneur in the logging industry in his own right. Not long after he began working for the mill company, he decided to buy timber of his own in the area. He worked hard for his employers in Port Blakely, but didn't plan to stay with them forever. The birth of his own logging company is described in *Lumber and Politics*:

> Toward the end of the 1880s he began buying timber, apparently with money borrowed from Captain Renton. In 1890, he resigned and set up S. G. Simpson and Company, with headquarters in the small Mason County town of Matlock.

However, Simpson's company remained closely connected with the Port Blakely Mill Company and in July 1893, cut seven million feet of logs, all destined for Port Blakely.

In 1895, Simpson, Alfred H. Anderson and four Port Blakely stockholders (likely the Renton and Ham estates, Holmes and Campbell) formed the Simpson Logging Company. Sol Simpson was the active force in this company, but two-thirds of its financing came from Port Blakely interests, and each shareholder received a sixth of the venture.

The Simpson Logging Company was thus something of a subsidiary of the Port Blakely Mill Company. Port Blakely had first claim on Simpson's logs and paid Simpson a lower price for its purchase of logs than it paid other suppliers. By 1898, Simpson had 500 men working in eight camps along eighty miles of railroad.

Simpson chafed under the restrictions the Port Blakely Mill Company placed on him, and finally could stand the situation no longer. In 1902, he informed Port Blakely that he had 'taken the liberty to advance the price of logs to the Blakely Mill to the same as other mill companies are paying'.

The terminating of its favored treatment by Simpson didn't terminate the business relationship between his company and Port Blakely. As happened twelve years earlier, when Simpson resigned from The Blakely Line and established S.G. Simpson Company, the two companies continued to work together. More and more, though, Simpson was absorbed in his own enterprises. Before he turned the business over to his son-in-law, Mark E. Reed, Sol Simpson had given a solid start to the company that was to become and remain a major factor in the forest products industry; a company that we know today as the Simpson Timber Company.

Port Blakely's timber holdings in Mason County eventually grew to more than 100,000 acres, and that acreage is still being managed today by its successor, Port Blakely Tree Farms.

ॐ

CHAPTER ELEVEN

SOME OTHER RESIDENTS OF THE 1880S: THE PETERSONS OF SUNNY HILL DAIRY AND AUGUST MATTSON

The immigrants who arrived at Port Blakely and elsewhere on Bainbridge Island during the 1880s were no more inclined to leave a record of just what made them locate there than the ones who came earlier or later. They just plain didn't have time to talk about it, didn't want to talk about it or weren't interested in looking back over their shoulders. But in spite of that, there were some whose stories survived the years.

Jons Petter Pettersson, like Gus Sanders and the Elofsons, was an early Swedish immigrant to Port Blakely. He arrived in San Francisco at the age of twenty, and seven years later, in 1883, homesteaded his Sunny Hill Dairy Farm above Blakely Harbor. He settled right in, began to slash brush—which suggests the mill company had logged this land some years before—and began his house, which he later valued at $75. At the land office in Olympia, his name was changed slightly, possibly by mistake, and he became Jons Peter Petersson. Later still, the family name became Peterson.

Jons' future wife, Johanna, had an experience familiar to many immigrants. Johanna left Sweden and arrived in New York at age sixteen in 1881, expecting to find her brothers there to meet her. They weren't, and there is nothing more in the family records about them. She had to go to a Swedish settlement house for temporary refuge. Quite on her own, she signed on with Captain August Mattson and his wife on the captain's ship, *Harvest Home*, to look after the couple's children on the ships voyage from New York to Port Blakely. In Port Blakely, she met Jons.

Johanna and Jons were married in 1887. By then Jons was able to say his home was worth $800. In addition, he had two horses, eight cows, six steers and four pigs. Soon the couple had two children, but the first died at about age one. Pioneer life for the immigrants of this period was straightforward and spartan and must have been almost unbearable at times.

The homestead lay at the head of a trail running up the hill on the south side of the millpond. The easiest ascent was to follow the east bank of a creek that drained a part of the farm. They built their home on a hillock near the stream, and from it they could look to the south out over all their land.

Below and just to the east of the house, they built their

Jons Peterson's Sunny Hill Dairy. Photo courtesy of the Peterson's granddaughter, Florence Peterson Swanson.

barn. It was added to as the dairy herd grew and soon had three levels. It was a long, handsome building that spanned a seasonal stream. Frenchie, the bull, had his quarters at one end of the first level, so he could be near his Jersey, Holstein and Guernsey wives.

The farm was half a mile long, and its east end reached all the way to the wagon road that ran up the hill from the harbor to Nils and Fausta Elofson's place. I. P. Vinblaut, who later changed his name to Edward Windblad, lived adjacent to both the Elofsons and the Petersons.

The Petersons were generous to other Swedish immigrants who jumped ship or arrived in more conventional ways and wanted to make their home in Port Blakely. They built several cottages on the wooded northern slope of the farm, where the pasture stopped and the land dipped steeply down toward the harbor. They charged nothing for the occupancy of these cottages—or, more likely, shacks—as the newcomers looked for work in the mill and helped out on the farm.

One long-term resident was Charlie Dahlstrom from Sweden, who married a Bella Coola Indian. She became known to the neighbors as Aunt Annie. Annie did everything. She raised canaries and made blackberry wine. She crocheted, she sewed, she knitted. She dug clams and collected seaweed—and dried them both on a line over the stove in her shack. She made pilot bread, donuts and cookies. She made doll clothes. She loved children. As one of the Peterson's granddaughters commented, "She was a wonderful woman. She wore a big hat and always wanted me to call her Auntie. Her shack always smelled of clams, but that didn't bother us or Charlie."

The Peterson's Sunny Hill Dairy survived well into the 20th century. But fire, an ever growing Fort Ward, and changing dairy practices eventually caused its demise. Green pastures returned to woodland. Still, Peterson descendants continue to own some of the land their immigrant forebears homesteaded more than 100 years ago.

Captain August Mattson, on whose ship Johanna Peterson traveled from New York to Port Blakely, made many voyages out of Puget Sound. His name is most often linked to that of the bark *Harvest Home*, of which he was master and part owner.

A Watkins photo, looking down at row of houses from Hall's Hill. Photo courtesy University of Washington, Special Collections, Watkins 5246.

The *Harvest Home* was well known in the coastal trade, but her crew's reputation was made in the summer of 1875, when she happened to be in port in Seattle. A longboat race in Elliott Bay was planned, and Mattson entered his ship's longboat with some of his crew as oarsmen. The *Harvest Home* entry won, and a silver tea service, provided by the merchants of Seattle, was the prize.

In 1879 Captain Mattson married Charlotte Nelson-Rehn, daughter of a prominent Swedish family, on the deck of the *Harvest Home* while she was anchored in Seattle. Ships in the harbor flew flags and put out bunting for the wedding. The sea captain immediately took his bride to sea, and their first child, named, appropriately enough, Neptune, was born on board in 1880. Two years later, the *Harvest Home* was lost in a storm north of the mouth of the Columbia River. All on board survived.

That year, Mattson built a house on Bainbridge Island, choosing a spot just outside of Gus Sanders' farm on Restoration Point. It was a large two-story structure such as a successful captain should have. With his family moved in, Mattson went to sea again, this time as skipper of the San Francisco-owned *Ella*

Carleton Watkins "dark room" tent shows in the foreground of this 1882 picture. The track is coming from the mill in the background to the shipyard which is just behind the photographer. Photo courtesy University of Washington, Special Collections, Watkins 5247.

S. Thayer. She was lost in a great storm off Cape Flattery in 1886. The captain reported the weather was the roughest he'd ever seen. Undeterred, he returned to the sea, sailing to Australia and South America for the next twenty-seven years without serious incident. He retired to his Restoration Point home and lived there until his death in 1924.

Benjamin S. Ryder was another early resident on the south side of Port Blakely harbor. He established a "questionable enterprise" on the shore about opposite Blakely Point. It and the few houses around it came to be known as Ryderville. His was at first the only two-story house in Ryderville. It was not only his home but also a tavern. The location proved to be a good one for a tavern. When the lumber wharves in the harbor became crowded with ships, other ships waiting their turn to load generally anchored alongside log booms, just off of Ryderville.

Sometimes two or more ships were moored bow-to-stern along the booms, which were waiting to be towed into the mill pond. The shore side of the log booms rested on the beach below the front door of the tavern. To crew members, the several attractions of Ryder's establishment were irresistible.

Ryderville customers were frequently rowdy and parents in the mill town warned their children not to go near the place. A later owner of the tavern, a man named Mike Lyons, was killed over a dispute regarding property lines.

The Ryderville tavern wasn't the only one to have problems with its reputation. Kitsap County commissioner proceedings of the time show that Annie Maloney of another Port Blakely tavern failed to get her liquor license renewed. She was not, the commissioners decided, "a proper person to have such a license".

With the arrival of the railroads in Seattle, more and more supplies came to Port Blakely from the city. They were brought from Seattle by the steamer *Michigan* or later the *Sarah M. Renton*. On their return trip, the steamers took farm produce from the island to markets in the city.

By the mid-1880s, Captain James Nugent offered three round trips a day to Seattle aboard the passenger steamer *Michigan*. The fare each way was $.50.

Shoppers from the mill town sometimes boarded the *Michigan* and went to the city to look for bargains, which upset mill company storekeeper, Thomas H. Brooks. Why, the company store even had a porter, Charles Marr, to help the ladies with their bags. Brooks couldn't see why anybody should go to Seattle to shop!

Until 1889, when Dr. Cecil Kellam established his practice at Port Blakely, medical attention was available in the town only on occasion. A number of families, including the Rentons, had established connections with doctors in Seattle, and they depended on the steamer to get them there.

The Renton's doctor was Dr. D. L. Smith, who had his office in the Colman Building on the waterfront. The building had been built by James M. Colman, who had purchased Renton's Port Orchard mill in 1864. For Bainbridge islanders, the location was very convenient. Sometimes Dr. Smith visited patients on the steamer at the dock in Seattle ($2.50 per visit), and sometimes he took the steamer to Port Blakely to make a house call

($20). Prescriptions came from A. B. Stewart on Seattle's Front Street (fourteen leeches for $2.35) and from Hasbrouck and Terry, also on Front Street (kidneywort for $.50). There was another pharmacist, Mathew A. Kelly, on Commercial Street. He billed the Rentons several times in July and August of 1886 for a mysterious ointment in 6 and 12 ounce mixtures. Someone in the family may have strayed into the poison oak that grows near Blakely Point.

 è

CHAPTER TWELVE

CALAMITY, THEN THE BIRTH
OF THE GREAT MILL

The caption of an article in the *Seattle Post-Intelligencer* for Saturday, February 4, 1888, proclaimed the calamity, and the article caught the drama of one of Port Blakely's darkest days.

DESTRUCTION OF BLAKELY MILLS

Yesterday morning, shortly after 8 o'clock, Port Blakely was visited by a destructive conflagration, which will cut a very important figure in that port's history, as it swept away one of the largest and best mills on Puget Sound... The fire is supposed to have originated from a hot journal box of the main engine... The flames were communicated to the belting which ran through the mill, and it did not take long for the fine dust, which ignites like powder, to envelope the entire building. The rapidity with which the fire swept through the building was something wonderful. So swift was the rush of the fire that many of the occupants of the mill had to jump from windows and slide down the gangways and log chutes to escape with their lives.

The company's steamer, *Politkofsky*, being in port, performed good service, throwing two streams of water on the flames... Mr. J. A. Campbell assumed charge and directed the bucket brigade, which worked with a will. The wind, fortunately, was blowing in shore, thus, saving the shipping in the harbor and giving their masters time to haul their vessels out into the stream. The building was covered with corrugated iron, which confined the flames and prevented the spread of the fire to buildings adjoining. The machine shops, although scorched, were saved. There were many willing hands to assist, and a good deal of lumber was saved.

A look through the blackened ruins showed the havoc the flames had made. Shafting, machinery and engines were twisted into all manner of shapes. It is thought that one of the engines and one of the gang saws can be repaired.

A reporter called on Captain Renton who remained in his office, and, although deprived of his eyesight, directed all the movements of the men and of the shipping, and was thoroughly conversant with all that was going on. He stated that the loss would reach $250,000, and that the company would immediately rebuild the mill, even if it had to hew out the lumber for doing so. It will be built in about the same location as the old mill.

About 260 men were employed in and about the mill. A great many of them will be retained to clear away the debris and to assist in the rebuilding. It will be fully four months before the company will be all equipped for business, but lumber will be cut in the new mill inside of 60 days.

A few supplemental notes followed the story:

Miss Jessie Livingston (Sarah Renton's granddaughter) is deserving of praise for the manner in which she catered at the Cookhouse to the wants of the Seattle firemen from Engine Co. No. 2. They came over from Seattle on a scow in tow of the tug *Tyee*... Captain Reynolds of the ship *Prussia* was noticed hard at work... The flames swept through the mill like a prairie fire, driving everything before them... There is enough lumber saved to load the *Fannie Dutard* and the *R. K. Ham*... The company may take the McDonald and Reitze mill and run it until their new one is ready for operation.

In Port Gamble, twenty miles down the Sound, people watched the red glow to the south and had a good idea of what had happened and to which mill. W. H. Talbot, one of the owners of the Port Gamble mill, had a higher estimate of the loss than was given by Captain Renton. He thought the loss "would squeeze" $500,000, if one included the loss of business. Later, Renton told Talbot's associate, Cyrus Walker, "the only thing that could have saved the mill was to have immersed it in Puget Sound".

Fire was the fear of every sawmill owner. One could be started by a hot journal box or by some other mechanical problem. Since the Port Blakely Mill had electric lights as early as 1882, there was no longer the danger of an upset "teakettle lamp" fueled by fish oil starting a fire. Sparks from ever-burning slab and waste wood fires were a constant worry.

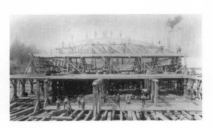

Late spring, 1888. Photo courtesy University of Washington, Special Collections, Watkins 4943.

The many hazards caused insurance premiums to be prohibitively high, and the mill was not insured. The fact that it had lasted from 1863 to 1888, twenty-five years, probably demonstrates the Captain's safety standards and the attention his men paid to potential hazards in the mill. There was a strict prohibition against smoking on any part of the sawmill or wharf property.

The *Post-Intelligencer* reporter was right in saying that the fire "cut a very important figure" in Port Blakely's history. It did so not by destroying a mill, but by making way for what would soon be described not as the largest sawmill on the West Coast, but as the largest in the world.

Captain Renton's statements to the reporter, the day of a fire that many would have viewed as disastrous, were not mere bravado. He had seen trouble before and risen above it.

Construction on the new mill began immediately after the fire, and Renton and John Campbell not only insured the new mill, but also took steps to see that the best in fire protection equipment was installed. Their attention to that detail has left a wonderful, unexpected record of the plan of the new "Great

Mill". Lodged as Sheet 36 of the Sanborn Fire Insurance Maps of Seattle for 1888 is one that doesn't seem to belong there at all. It holds a plan of the mill, the caption of which reads:

PORT BLAKELY SAW MILL
Renton Holmes and Co. Owners
8 miles from Seattle on W. Side of Sound
In Operation but not Fully Completed Aug. 1888
Building Substantial, Premises Tidy

An accompanying detailed description was written with the fire insurance purposes of the map in mind, but it also gives a vivid picture of the mill.

Building constructed on firm foundation of piling and solid ground. Timbers all heavy and little combustible material attached. Corrugated iron roof, sides and ends open. Double run of saws with capacity when completed of 300,000 feet per day. Rough lumber manufactured only at present. Average 200 hands. No lights. Work daytime only. Three night watchmen. Clock station in boiler room. 15 minute rounds...270,000 gallon reservoir on hill filled with salt water from harbor by No. 3 Knowles pump. 47 barrels with pails distributed through the mill...

The description cites fire extinguishers, a system of pipes, and 850 automatic sprinkler heads set ten feet apart. Hydrants were supplied with water from the reservoir, but they could be disconnected from that source and supplied with water from the bay, with the help of steam pumps. The sprinkler system came in for a share of praise from the newspapers of the day, but there is no record of it ever being put to the test other than one time during the next eighteen years.

The operation at Port Blakely was often referred to in the plural: "the mills at Port Blakely". At first this seems odd, but pictures as well as the plan of the mill show there were two log ways that carried logs from the log pond up to the main floor of the mill. Inside the single building, there were two sides to the mill, each capable of carrying out the full conversion of a log

Rebuilding of the mill, 1888. Photo courtesy Puget Sound Maritime Historical Society, Williamson Collection.

to lumber. The two sides could be operated at the same time or independently, thus allowing one side to be run while the other side was closed down for maintenance.

The mill floor and ship loading wharf around it were shown to be eight feet above the high tide level, as was the wooden wharf on which the mill office and all the associated buildings were located. These included a building housing the forge shop and woodworking machinery, another housing the pattern warehouse and sail loft, and others for storage, the general store, the freight house, the freight warehouse and the hay warehouse. Within the woodworking machinery building was the barley crusher room, still essential for the preparation of horse, livestock and chicken feed.

Bay Street, which ran in front of most of the houses on the north side of the harbor, was at an elevation of 15 feet and the backyards of the houses were about 20 feet above the high tide level. The houses are shown as being back from the shore between 50 and 100 feet.

The sawmill straddled the peninsula of land that led from the north shore to the log-pond dike and gate. The main mill building was 100 feet wide and extended 440 feet from west to east, beginning at a point about 40 feet into the log pond. Beyond it on the west were the two log ways extending still further into the log pond. Beyond the east end of the building were the lumber platform and the track for the carts to carry the lumber to the lumber wharf and the more distant shipyard. The planked lumber wharf extended 350 feet east into the har-

The completed mill, in production, about 1890. The waste burner, under construction—seen against the center of the mill—will replace the former waste burning site on the south shore. The waste burner was 76 feet high. Photo courtesy Puget Sound Maritime Historical Society, Williamson Collection.

bor from the end of the main building. From the west end of the log ways to the east end of the wharf, the entire structure was over 900 feet long. At its eastern face, the lumber loading wharf was about 225 feet wide; ships could also be loaded along much of the nearly 700-foot south side of the wharf that paralleled the mill.

On the north side of the sawmill was the boiler house. It was a building about 60 feet wide along the end nearest the sawmill and about 130 feet in length. It contained three 300-horsepower boilers. Steam from these boilers was delivered to six steam engines; these ran the gears and shafts that, using belts, ran all the mill's machinery. The sawdust used to fire the boilers was delivered on a conveyor from the mill. Water for the boilers was held in a 20,000-gallon tank just to the west of the boiler house, and this supply was backed up by a 200,000-gallon reserve tank at the north end of the building. The boiler house and the two adjacent water tanks, as well as the sawmill, were all on the peninsula at the south end of which was the gate between the harbor and the log pond.

One hundred feet short of the east end of the building, an inclined platform extended about 250 feet to the north. On it were two refuse trains (endless chains), which carried waste from the mill to the burn piles. Once lighted, they are said not to have gone out for years. The fires had a 25-foot-high brick and stone wall shielding the mill from them and were so bright their glow was seen for miles. Seattle residents pointed out the glow and smoke from across the water, and pilots sometimes used the fires as a beacon from out on the Sound.

If the platform just mentioned had been extended another 220 feet, it would have been at the front door of the cookhouse, where mill workers ate. Sounds like a pretty smoky location, but everyone in town was used to smoke—the Public and Society Hall, more commonly known as the Masonic Hall, was very close to the cookhouse. The dining room of the cookhouse was 200 feet long from west to east and 30 feet wide. On the side away from the mill was a good-sized kitchen. Off to the west were two hog houses, one only 25 feet from the corner of the dining room.

No dormitories are shown on the insurance map. They were to the west of the mill and on the north side of the log pond. Fifteen houses are shown, all but one of them in a row along Bay Street. All these houses, as well as the enlarged Bainbridge Hotel, were built in the early 1880s. One was two stories tall, the others were one-and-a-half-story structures. The two-story house was in about the middle of the row, close to the post office and the general store, which were on the wharf. There was one duplex in the group, farther to the east. Captain Renton's home was one of the two at the west end of the row, near the Masonic Hall. These two were the largest homes in town. The other was first occupied by hotel manager Daniel Sackman and his wife, Elizabeth, Mrs. Renton's daughter.

Central in the long row of houses was the Bainbridge Hotel. The insurance map shows it as a great rambling affair. The two-story structure faced the harbor over Bay Street; steps rose from the street to a 30-foot-long porch at the center of the building. Across the lobby from the hotel entrance was the entrance to a comfortably large dining room. A breezeway extended from the dining room north to a group of rooms that contained the kitchen, a woodshed and a laundry room, where the mapmaker noted there was a kettle on a stove. Near the kitchen was a small building marked "sleeping rooms", probably for the Chinese cooks, and just beyond it, a hen house. Off the lobby of the Bainbridge Hotel to the east was the saloon. There was also a storage building near the hotel. It was quite a complex.

The livery and feed building was across Bay Street and just east of the hotel. When steamers landed in front of the hotel, visitors had only to cross the wharf to find their accommodations. If they were going farther, the livery man was right at hand.

With its modern amenities, Port Blakely became a comfortable destination for visitors to the frontier and for tourists from the burgeoning city of Seattle across the water. Of course, Seattle was a destination for Port Blakely people as well, for while the mill town was concentrating on it single industry, Seattle was developing into an eclectic center of commerce.

It is appropriate to close this chapter about the calamity that befell Port Blakely and the rebuilding that followed in 1888, with a further reference to Seattle. If Port Blakely was important to Seattle, and vice versa, they also had something else in common. In 1888, people in Seattle watched in awe as the Port Blakely mill burned. Just a little over a year later, on the afternoon of June 5, 1889, Bainbridge islanders were mesmerized by a sight even more spectacular and disastrous: the great Seattle fire. Helped by a wind straight out of the north, the fire destroyed eighty acres of business blocks and about forty acres of wharves. For a city of only 40,000 people, that was a devastating loss. Nils Elofson and his family and neighbors, unable to help save it, sat on the top of Mosebacke, the high point of the Elofson farm, and watched Seattle burn.

સ⮾

CHAPTER THIRTEEN

THE MAN WITH THE BLACK
BAG, DR. CECIL KELLAM

Port Blakely's population boomed in the 1880s, first with the establishment of the shipyard and later with the rebuilding of the sawmill. The number of residents of the little town more than tripled—to nearly 1,000—by the end of the decade, and all those newcomers needed places to live, better service to Seattle, a larger school—and someone to patch them up when they were injured or sick.

There had been resident doctors in town before, but their stays proved to be short, throwing citizens back on their own resources. Sicknesses were dealt with by using mustard plasters and other family remedies. To treat injuries, doctors came from Seattle by steamboat or from Port Madison overland. In the 1870s, a Dr. Arnold served the entire Port Blakely, Port Madison, Port Orchard area.

The town's clear need for a resident doctor came to the attention of Cecil Corydon Kellam, a young man at Willamette Medical School in Portland, Oregon. Born in Buckton in upstate New York on May 1, 1865, Kellam had come to Portland because his uncle was on the faculty of the medical school. He enrolled in the class of 1889, graduated with twelve other doctors on April 1, 1889, and became the first secretary of the medical school alumni association. He liked the West, and the opportunity at Port Blakely appealed to him, so upon graduation in 1889, he moved to Port Blakely and established his practice.

Dr. Kellam was the answer to many a prayer. He served Port Blakely for forty years, operating out of an office in the heart of the community, close to the homes, the ships and the mill from which his patients came.

After his first two years in practice, Dr. Kellam returned to his home in New York State to persuade Jessie Myra Lang, the daughter of a leading family in Brasher Falls near Buckton, to marry him. She agreed, and after the wedding, the two lived in New York City while the doctor took graduate training at Bellevue Hospital. Dr. Kellam was a slender, handsome young man with a fine straight nose and a bushy moustache. A few hearts must have been broken when he returned to Port Blakely with a wife.

Jessie was a sophisticated young lady, and one can only speculate on her reaction to the community of immigrants, boisterous ships' crews, the winter-long rain and mud, and the noise and smoke of the mill itself. At times, she probably burst into tears.

The couple first lived in one of the houses east of the Bainbridge Hotel, and it was there that their first child, Cecil, Jr., was born. Later, the Kellams moved to a larger home that was part way up the hillside toward the school and fronted on a boardwalk along which were two other houses. A steep flight of stairs reached down from the walk to the center of the village below. From the houses, there was an unobstructed view of the busy harbor. Families living in them could see the ships that came in to load lumber as well as the company tugs that brought the big log rafts into the harbor from logging camps around the Sound. They could look down at the activity on Bay Street as well as on the wharf where the post office flag flew, signaling that this rough outpost had connections with places more substantial.

During his many years of medical practice, Dr. Kellam delivered more than a generation of babies. His was a true family practice; many of his babies grew to be parents themselves and had their babies delivered by the good doctor. One hundred years after his arrival in Port Blakely, many people on Bainbridge Island still remember him with a respect bordering on devotion—as though he was nearly able to perform miracles.

He made house calls by foot, by carriage and, finally, in his Model T Ford. How comforting it must have been to a mother to look out her window to see the doctor coming up

Dr. C.C. Kellam in his office. Photo by Jessie Kellam.

to her house, and to the Elofson, Sanders, Peterson, Monk and other children to have the familiar face of the doctor leaning reassuringly over their beds. Dr. Kellam came to love the place. The couple had two more sons after Cecil, Jr., Louis Lang and Silas Sumner Kellam.

Jessie, though she seems to have tried, was never as keen about life in Port Blakely as her husband. The small town did not offer someone of her sensitivities much in the way of stimulation. She was a talented and creative person; she dressed with flair and made her own clothes. She was a good photographer and took many pictures of life on the harbor. She put some of them on a three-panel changing-room screen for her husband's office.

Dr. Kellam's black bag, with its many medical implements and its bottles, as well as the screen that was made for him by his wife, are now in the Bainbridge Island Historical Society Museum. The donor was Dr. Kellam's daughter-in-law, who gave them to the museum in April, 1984, after the death of her husband, Silas Sumner Kellam.

The Kellam boys all went to Port Blakely School, just a few steps away up the hill from their home. At one point, Dr. Kellam was secretary to the local school board.

One evening early in 1896, according to a surviving program, Jessie Kellam performed with other talent in town to put on a full evening of entertainment in the Masonic Hall. She was the star of the show. First, she played in a guitar duet and gave a vocal solo, "The Exiles Lament". She followed her first two appearances with a recitation titled "A Leap for Life." Then she sang "Gypsy Queen" in a vocal duet.

In later years, when the Ladies Auxiliary of the Presbyterian Church put together its *Port Blakely Cook Book*, "Mrs. Dr. Kellam" contributed a recipe. But cooking does not seem to have been a particular interest; most of the contributors had two or more recipes in the book, but she had only one. If she had enjoyed cooking, the recipe might have been a more exciting one than suet pudding. It was the stage that appealed to her, not cooking.

There were other good times, though. The family has a picture of the steamer *Favorite*, crowded with passengers in their best clothes, with this caption: "May 26, 1908—Lang and Sumner with Mama going to view the Atlantic Fleet". There were other things to do besides cook.

Dr. Kellam was an enterprising man as well as a good citizen and doctor. He developed a friendship with and confidence in Charles L. Morrill, who ran an early grocery store in West Blakely, and shortly after Hall Brothers shipyard moved from Port Blakely to Winslow in 1903, Morrill and Dr. Kellam became partners in that town's first drugstore. Called "Kellam and Morrill," it was in the business block on the west side of the ravine near Winslow's first post office. With this new venture, Dr. Kellam added Winslow to his medical territory. Dr. Frank Shepard established himself in Winslow in 1912, and the two men got along well. Dr. Shepard had the first car on the island and is said to have taught Dr. Kellam how to drive his Model T.

Dr. Kellam joined the medical corps of the Army in 1916 and was posted to Fort Ward on Bainbridge Island. He divided his hours between his patients in town and his patients at the fort. It was during this period that he worked night and day to save his patients who were hit hard by the Spanish Flu epidemic. He had little medicine to help them and is said to have relied on whiskey and quinine. It was a sad time for Port Blakely; once there were two funerals in one day. People wore flu masks and tried to avoid contact with sick people, and they depended on Dr. Kellam, sometimes to work miracles.

After the war, the doctor stayed in the Army reserves and later became a "major, auxiliary".

Jessie inherited money from her family and invested part of it in loans and in property on Bainbridge Island. Some of the borrowers defaulted and she later acquired their property in fulfillment of their obligation to her. These means, separate from those of her husband, gave Jessie the freedom to make a difficult decision.

Jessie Kellam at Blakely Point.

There is a picture of Jessie, in a stylish hooded cape, taken while she was standing beside the brown conglomerate rock of Blakely Point. The picture shows that she was a beautiful woman, but the pensive expression suggests that she was aloof and unhappy. She simply wasn't cut out for the rough mill town to which her marriage had brought her.

Jessie's feelings about Port Blakely eventually developed into an estrangement from her husband. This was in about 1920, at the time their second child reached high school age. Her condition could have been triggered by the emotional stress she suffered when their oldest son, Cecil, Jr., was badly injured by poison gas during the war, or it could have been that she finally rebelled against small town life and never having an identity separate from her husband. Whatever the reason, she moved to Seattle, taking their two younger sons with her. Neither she nor the doctor ever formally sought a separation, but for most of the rest of his life, Dr. Kellam lived alone at Port Blakely, and after the boys left the house, Jessie lived alone in Seattle.

After the departure of his wife and two sons, Dr. Kellam continued his practice from his office on Bay Street, but he moved from his residence to a room in the Bainbridge Hotel. He ate his meals there and played cards with other longtime male members of the community. He belonged to Evergreen Lodge No. 126 of the Independent Order of Oddfellows, as well as Renton Lodge No. 80, Knights of Pythias, both of Port Blakely, and he served as secretary of the Port Blakely Cemetery. Otherwise, he was never a very social person, though the warmth he showed a generation and half of patients has not been forgotten.

He was a quiet man who simply did his job well, and people from those days remember him as the doctor who took care of everybody. In return, after Jessie's departure, people at Port Blakely took care of him by inviting him over for meals. Katy Welfare Warner remembers that while everyone loved him, they felt sorry for him, too. She recalls:

> He was lonely, and you just knew he didn't have the kind of life, when he went home, that other people did.

In the late 1920s, when the economy was booming, Dr. Kellam got caught up in the period's speculative boom in greenhouses. He persuaded Seinosuke Takayoshi to manage the operation of several large greenhouses on the south-facing lower hillside above the road between Pleasant Beach and Point White. He built a house there for the Takayoshis and one for himself, to which he moved when the Bainbridge Hotel burned in 1928. For a short time, he was joined at Pleasant Beach by his son, Cecil, Jr., and his family. Cecil, Jr. was a living tragedy of the war. He suffered recurring illnesses and was unable to earn a living. The burden of holding together the young Kellam family, Cecil III and a daughter, fell on Cecil Jr.'s wife, Mae. Before long, they left Bainbridge, moved to Vermont and then New York, leaving Dr. Kellam alone again.

The speculative boom of the 1920s ended with the Great Depression of the 1930s, and with it, Dr. Kellam's greenhouse business collapsed.

He moved to Seattle to live on Belmont Avenue, near Jessie, and died in 1934. Dr. Kellam was buried in the Port Blakely Cemetery. Hundreds of his friends and grateful patients came to his service to say farewell to the man with the black bag, the good doctor, on whom they had depended for so long.

ॐ

CHAPTER FOURTEEN

THE LIVES OF CAPTAIN AND MRS. RENTON ARE REVIEWED AND PRAISED, AND THE MOURNING OF THEIR DEATHS BY HOSTS OF FRIENDS IS RECOUNTED

From the day in 1863 when Captain Renton moved to Blakely Harbor from Port Orchard, his mill town grew outward like the ripples from a pebble thrown into the water. As the mill and wharf came alive with the sounds of men, saws and ships, its uplands began to ring with shouts of children on their way to school or going about their chores. The rough-and-tumble mill town became a community, and in the center of it, like the stolid grandparents in an old family portrait, stood Captain Renton and his wife, Sarah.

The Captain described himself at the age of sixty-four as "stout and fleshy"; he weighed 220 pounds. The *Seattle Post-Intelligencer* at one point said that his "strong, clear features, set off with steel gray hair and whiskers, told of his indomitable will". One of Carleton Watkin's pictures, which included the Captain and several other men standing in front of the company store in 1882, does convey this image. How nearly that indomitable will came to being broken after the explosion at Port Orchard and again during his early days at Port Blakely. Children in Port Blakely in the 1880s must have loved getting a glimpse of the portly town founder as he walked along the planked wharves. Adding to the drama was the fact that they

Captain Renton, in front of the company store and office, to the left of the man with the stick. Photo courtesy University of Washington, Special Collections, Watkins 5236.

could watch him, but he couldn't see them—he was completely blind. They must have been fascinated to see how he made his way about the mill and the town unassisted, depending on his legendary memory to help him "see" his way around.

He held on to the mystique of the seagoing life, too, always referring to himself as "captain" even though he hadn't sailed a ship in years.

By the time the "largest sawmill in the world" was completed at Port Blakely in 1888, the Rentons were in their 70s. The Captain still went daily from his home to the mill office, wearing his usual cardigan jacket and round slouch hat. He would often sit on a covered bench in front of the office and "watch" what went on on the wharf.

Though he was getting older, Renton is said to have known the quality of all the timber on the mill company's many landholdings, how much finished lumber it would produce and in what condition the land would be once the trees were cut. He stayed current on every aspect of the business, wheeling and dealing in lumber, politics, labor problems and a roller coaster economy.

Renton was the kind of man who believed that people should make their own way, and he was not sympathetic to some labor demands of the mill workers and loggers. But he never had the reputation of being an exploitive man; in fact, he was considered generous, and it was said his employees never hesitated to ask his help when in need. He gave to worthy causes as well as to people. One early gift was lumber for the construction of "the Brown Church" at Second Avenue and Madison Street in the spring of 1865.

In Seattle, Captain Renton was looked upon as a shrewd investor, but also as a man who kept his word no matter what. He invested heavily in real estate, one tract later being divided up to become the blocks surrounding 23rd Avenue East and East Union Street. The part of the city where East Madison Street crosses 16th Avenue East was, for many years, called Renton Hill. It was one of the few Seattle landforms, other than Denny Hill, to be named for a local pioneer.

He invested in coal mines and in railways—and often saved the day for entrepreneurs of those projects. His help and interest were recognized, as noted earlier, when the town of Renton was named for him in 1876. He and Mrs. Renton were sought out as investors in a variety of other enterprises. One of them was the Boston National Bank of Seattle. When it was organized on July 10, 1889, Renton as well as his old friend and competitor, Cyrus Walker, were named directors.

Most of his adult life, Renton was plagued with failing sight, and he went to many doctors hoping for a cure. But he apparently never complained about being blind—in fact, his friend C. T. Conover, longtime Seattle realtor and historian, said he was the "least handicapped blind person" he'd ever seen.

Sarah, some said, was just as astute in business matters as her husband. "They operated as a team", Conover said. "The Captain consulted her in all his dealings and their money was handled as if from 'one purse'".

Sarah was a peacemaker who helped the poor, the Indians, hospitals in financial trouble and other worthy causes, Conover said in an article in the *Seattle Times*. "She was never idle".

Shortly after the new mill was completed in 1888, the mill company launched a passenger vessel named for Sarah. The 137-ton, 92-foot-long propeller-driven steamer *Sarah M. Renton* provided the town of Port Blakely with scheduled passenger and freight service to Seattle. Sarah Renton and her husband were to celebrate their 50th wedding anniversary in August 1891, and the naming of the vessel for Sarah in 1889 must have been in anticipation of this occasion. It may also have been recognized that Sarah would not live to celebrate the anniversary. She died at Port Blakely on May 12, 1890, at the age of seventy-four and was buried on the west side of Seattle's prestigious Lakeview Cemetery on Capitol Hill.

Her grave is marked by the family monument on which, in addition to her name and the dates of her life, is this rather odd inscription: "Erected by her daughters". There is no mention of Renton having joined them in placing the monument, one hopes because it wasn't erected until after his death.

For some time before Sarah's death, Renton's step- granddaughter, Clara Martha Livingstone (Mrs. Frank W. Clayton) managed the Renton household. But with Sarah gone, the old house was torn down, and the Captain moved into the Port Blakely home of his sister, Mrs. John Campbell, Sr.. She (Mary Renton Campbell) and her husband had moved from Pictou to Port Blakely only three years earlier in 1887, after Captain Campbell retired from a forty-nine-year career with Cunard Lines. Margaret Renton Campbell and her husband, William, had also moved to Port Blakely.

While the years had taken their toll on Renton, and after Sarah's death life must have lost a great deal for him, 1891 held one thrill that must have brought a warm smile. If it hadn't already earned its right to the title of "The Largest Sawmill in the World" Renton's new Port Blakely mill did for the year 1890. That year, 105 heavily loaded lumber ships left its docks. When the figures for other mills on the Sound were gathered, it was determined that the entire Puget Sound lumber fleet shipped a total of 430 cargoes. The thrill was that nearly a quarter of them had left from Port Blakely and that the next largest shipper was the Port of Tacoma, which reported the departures of seventy-one ship loads of lumber for the year. Renton must have reveled hearing the mill running night and day, been pleased for his sister and her son, John Campbell, who had measured up to his expectations, and marveled at the thought of there being as many as a dozen ships at a time tied up at his wharves.

Captain Renton died of peritonitis at his sister's home on July 18, 1891. His illness was a short one. True to form, he is said to have been in consultation about mill business on the day of his death.

In the newspapers, his friends praised the sea Captain turned lumberman as a "great big, noble, manly man". One friend said, "He was strictly just to all, and yet he had a warm, kindly heart".

The mill closed for three days when its founder died, and the papers described in great detail the sorrow of his employees and friends. In flowery prose, the *Seattle Press-Times* referred to him as "the mighty oak, fallen from the forest of human lives".

The day Renton was buried was a sad one in Port Blakely. The mill was quiet, the ships in the harbor draped in black crepe. Town residents walked about "listlessly". The Campbell's house was draped with black and white streamers. In the front room, the Captain lay in state, in a handsome black casket with silver side-bars. A glass top covered the upper part of the coffin, and a reporter was obviously moved at the sight of Renton: "...the sturdy massive face, strong even in death, bearing an expression of countenance as resolute as ever animated it in life, and the only visible indication of submission to the dread inevitable being found in the quiet arms peacefully crossed on the stilled breast".

In an adjoining room, the mourners gathered. They included Seattle pioneer A. A. Denny, Henry Hall and his son James Hall of the shipyard, Cyrus Walker of Pope & Talbot, and George A. Meigs of Port Madison. The reporter estimated at least 1,000 people filled the house, the yard and the street for the short service. Port Blakely Masonic Lodge members marched to the house in uniform; the choir, accompanied by organist Josephine Plate, sang some hymns and "many silent tears were seen to flow from strong men long since strangers to the feeling".

The pallbearers, many of them well along in years, had some trouble getting the casket to the wharf because of the great weight of the Captain. The tide was out, but they managed to get it down the gangplank and aboard the *Politkofsky*. A flotilla of seven boats, each heavily draped in mourning, with flags at half-mast, were led out of Port Blakely by the steamer *Sarah M. Renton*.

Met in Seattle by throngs of Masons, the cortege and the casket were taken in a parade of carriages to the Methodist Protestant Church, where an additional service was held. Captain Renton's long time friend, Rev. John F. Damon, officiated. There were 135 carriages, cabs and buggies in the procession to Lakeview Cemetery, where Renton was buried in the family plot.

The south side of the family monument simply records the dates of his birth and death, nothing more. It seems inadequate; the *Press-Times* did a better job of eulogizing Renton when it said, "The strong man was gone, but the stern philosophy of his life had put life into the commerce of Puget Sound that will insure for him an imperishable monument".

Sarah's two living daughters, Mary Gaffney and Elizabeth Sackman, seem to have felt for some time that they weren't getting fair treatment from their stepfather. Their mother's estate, in excess of $1 million, was left to them, but after Captain Renton's death, they contested his will, which dealt with his $3 million estate. Renton named his nephews, not his wife's daughters as inheritors of his mill company fortune. The sisters argued, in a lawsuit, that Renton had used money their mother inherited from her first husband to start the company. Therefore, they should inherit a portion of their stepfather's mill company interests.

There was a mild flurry of interest in the case in Seattle papers, one calling it "a skeleton in the closet", but the case was dismissed by the Superior Court as not being "definite" enough. The daughters appealed, but the state Supreme Court upheld the lower court's decision, and no more was heard. Renton had never legally adopted Sarah's daughters, though they assumed his name.

With the final illness of Captain Renton, and then his death, the full responsibility of managing the mill rested on the shoulders of his nephew John A. Campbell. He had fully measured up to his uncle's assessment of him, as expressed in those early letters to John's uncle, William Campbell, almost twenty years before.

ॐ

CHAPTER FIFTEEN

HEYDAYS ON THE HARBOR

It was an impressive place, this town that the Captain had built. The mill and the harbor must have been the inspiration for scores of effusive lyric letters sent to people back home, but the words of newspaper reporters who were similarly moved are the best on-the-spot records of the place. They tried to catch the feel of Port Blakely, and some did it very well.

> Port Blakely, the site of the world renowned Port Blakely Mill, is one of the busiest and most thriving towns on the Pacific Coast, and the throb of the ponderous machinery is manifest both day and night. The noise of the whirring wheels, the heavy pulsations of the many engines and the incessant hum of the saws and the planers impress a person with the feeling that these are all a part of a gigantic living being and not mechanical devices that are controlled by human beings. The precision of movement of the men as they work along the wharves and among the maze of ships impresses a person with the feeling that they are a part and parcel of the machinery whose throbbing is felt in all parts of the town.
>
> A reporter from the *Press-Times* was detailed yesterday [Friday, April 5, 1895] to visit this busy colony and he embarked

Ships loading lumber, circa 1900. Photo courtesy Library of Congress.

on the steamer *Sarah M. Renton* at 10 o'clock A.M. In just 40 minutes, the steamer, under the excellent command of Captain W. H. Primrose, covered the distance of nine miles and landed its passengers at the dock at Port Blakely. The day was pleasant and the trip was a most pleasing one, the boat running as smoothly as an ocean liner. Everything was neat and comfortable, probably cleaner and better kept than on any other steamer on the Sound.

Port Blakely is admirably situated for a mill site, it consisting of a cove or inlet sufficiently large to accommodate two score of deep water vessels at the same time, and yet leave sufficient room for the booming of many logs. When the steamer *Renton* got in yesterday morning, there were 15 deep water vessels taking in lumber for coast and foreign ports, or else preparing to do so. Their masts and spars rose in bewildering confusion and looked like a miniature forest. . .

The town of Port Blakely is an interesting spot. The principal road [Bay Street] runs parallel with the waterfront and along it are built neat cottages and two-story houses, which the mill rents to its employees for a nominal sum... Up the side and on the roof of each house are ladders to be used in case of fire. Some of the larger houses have three ladders, but there is not a house in town belonging to the company that has not at least two. All over the property covered by the mill are numerous signs prohibiting smoking, and it is an order that is never allowed to be violated by either workman or stranger. The town has a church and a public

Action on the wharf of the second mill: ship __Mercury__ loading timbers; slab wood ready for the steamers; passengers waiting for the boat to Seattle. Photo courtesy Puget Sound Maritime Historical Society, Williamson Collection.

school, and the inhabitants appear to be thoroughly happy.

The location of this 1895 church has not been determined. The reporter's reference was probably to the Masonic Hall, where church services were held, for, as yet, there was no church building in town.

Writing the next year in the *Seattle Evening Times*, a "stringer" living in Port Blakely commented on some different aspects of the community in this article dated September 15, 1896:

Last Saturday was the monthly payday for the employees of the Port Blakely Mill Company. Fifteen thousand dollars and more were distributed among the men, and a very interesting spectacle it was. All day long and into the evening the cashier was kept busy. The men get fair wages and are liberal with their money, this fact attracting each month dozens of agents, peddlers and salesmen to our port. Men come representing every kind of goods and ware, and it is very interesting to watch and hear these fellows with their glib tongues present their articles to the employees as they come from the cashier's office. The theater parties, elocutionists and other performers too, seem to strike the place just after this important time; and well they know when it comes, perhaps even better than the workman himself...

Politics do not seem to be a matter of discussion, as in other places where there are idle men to take up the matter. For men who work from 7 in the morning until 6 at night, by the time dinner is over and the paper read, the evening has nearly drawn to a close... Nearly 200 of the Seattle daily papers find their way here.

The company, besides her mill, has numerous well-equipped workshops. Her machine shop is about the best on the Sound, and she also has a large and well-arranged brass and iron foundry, where all the company work is done. The company has railroads, logging camps and steamboats, all of which send their repairing here, as this is the central place. The old steamer *Favorite*, which has just been put into commission, was entirely refitted and overhauled at the company's own shops.

We must not, in our sketch, forget the shipyard owned and operated by the Hall Bros. One steamer [the 229 ton steamer *Scray*, built for Hawaiian inter-island service] has been finished this year and another, the *Nueau*, is nearly finished and a schooner is well under way. The schooner will be the largest ever built on the coast. [This was the *Inca*.] Nearly 200 men are employed in the yard, receiving, on an average, $3 a day for their work.

The entertainment given by Mrs. Worthington in the Port Blakely Hall Saturday night was greatly appreciated by her audience.

Thomas Davenport, sailor on the British ship *Dundee*, died yesterday morning at 10:30. He had been troubled with his kidneys for some time, but they seemed to have gotten worse since the ship arrived in port.

The steamer *Fairhaven* came in yesterday morning, bringing ten tons of potatoes for the mill company.

These were the heyday years of Port Blakely. The shipyard and the mill were both busy. One hundred ninety-one vessels sailed from the port with a record 105 million board feet of lumber during 1895. That was more than an 80 percent increase

The band at Port Blakely. From l. to r.: Jimmie Hall (of the Hall Bros. shipyard family), Charlie McKinney, Harry Ziegler, William Frazer, unidentified, Adams Brant, Harry Burton, Ernie Mcdonald, Arnie Slater, Charlie Brook, John Husband. Athol Falt, and James Robinson are sitting. Photo courtesy Bainbridge Island Historical Society.

over the very substantial movement of 1890 that had so pleased Captain Renton. Almost as much lumber was shipped in 1896. In 1896 local mail delivery began. Mr. Benner made his mail delivery rounds with a wheelbarrow. The school's new second floor rooms were being used to capacity, and the play-yard was full at recess and after school.

Port Blakely was a patriotic town. When the steamship *Queen* arrived on the Sound bringing home the soldiers who had fought in the Spanish-American War, the mill company's *Favorite* was the first ship out in the stream to greet her.

The *Seattle Post-Intelligencer* often sent its reporters to Port Blakely. One of them, in April 1899, was especially taken with the ships in the harbor. In port, he said, were the *Fanny Dutard,* the *Challenger,* the *Repeat,* the *Excelsior,* the *Wawona,* the *Seminole,* the *Topgallant,* the *Kate Davenport,* the *Snow and Burgess* as well as the British bark *Dominion* and the huge British ships *Ancyra* and *Port Stanley.* They were bound, in addition to ports nearer at hand, for Sydney and Port Pirie, Australia; Delagoa Bay, South Africa; and Callao, Peru.

Having been put in a poetic mood by such names and

places, the reporter gave this colorful picture of what he saw before him:

> The great fleet presented an impressive and picturesque appearance yesterday as it rode quietly at the secure anchorage afforded in that sheltered arm of Puget Sound. The water was smooth as the face of a mirror. The great forest of masts showed up against an artist's sky of mottled clouds, whose nimbus masses were broken by streaks of genial April sunshine. Behind the port rose the wooded heights whose evergreen color makes them a scene of perpetual beauty. Long booms of logs lay like shoals along the surface of the bay. White-winged gulls sailed gracefully about the Harbor. A flock of crows was cawing noisily and darting about, now perching in the rigging of a schooner and anon flying after the proverbial crow fashion, straight away, as if on some distant errand. Far in the background peaks of the Olympics showed with softened blue and white and told of winter snows and forest depths. Nearer the water the long line of houses owned by the mill company bespoke the home life of the workingman. Central feature of all stood the giant mill, the largest in the world...

Just before the turn of the century, two major developments at Port Blakely gave a last boost to its economy. In 1898, a berthing slip for barges was built on the south side of the harbor. Tracks were laid from the grid iron on the berthing slip to a new planing mill and dry kiln, passing through the recently completed yard for the air-drying of lumber. The new facility enabled the great mill, which had previously cut for the cargo trade exclusively, to enter the eastern rail trade. It began loading lumber on railcars and sending these on barges holding nine cars each to the main railroad line in Seattle. The dry kiln sped the drying of green lumber and the finely equipped planing mill finished its surface and edges, enabling Port Blakely to compete most effectively in the rail trade market.

The other development, a telegraph crossarm factory, was built near the railroad barge berthing slip in 1899. With the rapid expansion of the telegraph and telephone systems around the country, the firm of Walworth and Neville of Bay City, Michigan, began manufacturing predrilled arms that carried glass insulators and were attached horizontally near the top of telegraph poles.

Buying raw material from its neighbor, the Blakely crossarm factory employed twenty men at the outset, with expectations that it would soon employ 200 and be the largest such plant in the country. Its product was loaded on railroad cars and shipped to Seattle, making good use of the port's new barge facility.

At the turn of the century, the mill was still managed by John Campbell, Captain Renton's nephew. A bachelor at age fifty-four, he was assisted by his brother James. A Seattle reporter described the two as "practical, capable and energetic lumbermen and businessmen and the right men in the right place".

The Campbells weren't the only ones who got high praise for their work in the company. Charles S. Holmes, now sixty-eight and still president of the company and manager in San Francisco, was considered "one of the best and shrewdest lumbermen on the Pacific Coast".

Holmes generally stayed in San Francisco but visited Port Blakely now and then. In 1899, he brought his eighteen-year-

Port Blakely about 1900. Hall Brothers' spar dock is on the left. Ships and second sawmill are still active. Thirty-two people and the horse can be seen on Bay Street. Photo courtesy Puget Sound Maritime Historical Society, Williamson Collection.

old daughter with him to the frontier town and wrote back to another daughter, Nellie, about the trip:

> My dear Nellie,
>
> I have just returned from a trip to Port Blakely and must write you a line of things there and of our trip. We had a good trip up on the cars and arrived at Seattle about 6 P.M. John Campbell met us and we went to the Rainier Grand Hotel. It was Sunday evening and we went to church and the next day went to Blakely, and as usual stayed at the James Campbell's...
>
> I was laid up about three days with a cold and no appetite. After I got better, we went up to the logging camps and this Gertie enjoyed very much. . . You will remember the lake in the woods where the camp was when you were there. There is now a large shingle mill built there belonging to the logging company, and cars go to the mill and load shingles for the eastern market. The logging now is a good many miles north of where it was when you were at camp.
>
> Seattle is a busy lively place. Also Blakely has much improved.

With glass plates and heavy cameras, it was possible to complement the written record with a record of another kind—photographs. Some of the earliest were taken in 1882 by the renowned San Francisco photographer Carleton Watkins. In the 1890s, there seems to have been an awareness among photographers as well as writers that before them at Port Blakely lay something not only tremendous and beautiful, but also passing. So they sought carefully to record it. These efforts reached their peak at the turn of the century. There were amateur photographers like Charles James Lincoln, Tamegoro Takayoshi and Jessie Kellam, who lived on the harbor and had the most frequent opportunities to catch it in all its moods. And there were professionals as well, like I.J. Webster and N. W. Stevens, whose firm of Webster and Stevens took pictures of almost every ship that entered the Sound. But, if Carleton Watkins took the best pictures of the town and the first mill in the 1880s, a man named Wilhelm Hester took the best pictures of Blakely Harbor and its ships and men during the heydays at the turn of the century.

An immigrant German, Wilhelm Hester had a special feeling for sailing ships and their crews. For about a decade, starting in 1895, he worked to make a living by taking pictures in lumber ports around the Sound in all seasons and in all kinds of weather. In 1906, he suddenly gave up professional photography, storing his glass plates in barrels in his Seattle

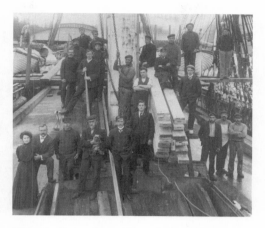

Wilhelm Hester photo of Captain Vought and his wife and crew on the ship Sierra Lucena at Port Blakely in 1904. Photo courtesy University of Washington, Special Collections.

home. A bachelor who turned a recluse, he neither dated nor identified his work. The plates were discovered in the early 1940s and identified and dated after years of painstaking work. They make up the best photographic record of turn-of-the-century Port Blakely.

As the century closed, John Campbell had this to say about the mill:

> The mill was never in better shape than it is today. We have just completed our annual repairs. While these are in progress we shut down one side of the mill and run the other side night and day. We have finished all repairs on both sides and are now running overtime. Business is good. During the winter, we had a shortage of logs, but our supply is ample now; not more than we want, but just enough...

It sounds as though John Campbell, even in times of prosperity, watched over the operation just as carefully as his uncle had. It was a matter of keeping things in balance, of being steady. John Campbell continued to be respected for that ability and that quality. ❧

CHAPTER SIXTEEN

KIMONOS, ICE CREAM AND MEMORIES: THE PEOPLE OF THE JAPANESE VILLAGES OF YAMA AND NAGAYA

For Chiye Shigemura Umezuka, memories of growing up in Port Blakely go far beyond board feet of lumber and boat launchings. She remembers searches for the *matsutake* (wild mushrooms) and warabi (edible fern) on the hillsides, New Year's Day celebrations and a mysterious haunted house.

She remembers a very special part of Port Blakely: the thriving Japanese settlement that grew there in the 1890s, transforming a logged-off hillside into a community where visitors could enjoy a Japanese meal, take a traditional Japanese bath and on special occasions, see women dressed in kimonos, looking for all the world as if they were in a Japanese village—not an American mill town.

"In the photographs, J-town (as it was sometimes called) may look like a shantytown, but to those of us who grew up in it, it was a great town", says Chiye.

The records suggest that the first person to emigrate from Japan to the Pacific Northwest was a seaman who came in 1888, but some say Japanese were present at Port Blakely in 1883. At any rate, by the time of the census in 1889, there were thirty-five Japanese men in Port Blakely. It is clear that the Japanese were relatively new to Port Blakely when the census was taken, for no Japanese names are used to identify them. Instead, they are listed with names such as Laughing Jap, Dwarf Jap, Mikado, and Talker, Chippy, Boots, and Stumpy, with their origin on the census simply shown as "Jap". Several Japanese were identified in mill lingo just by a number as "Jap 1" or "Jap 4". Maybe this simple way was the best way to start.

According to Kihachi Hirakawa who arrived in 1890, most of the seamen and other early immigrants arrived without passports but were not denied entry. Hirakawa, an educated man, has left the earliest account of the Japanese in Port Blakely. In his autobiography, he reflects on his youth in Japan, of his love for his family and his homesickness. But he writes that his family had been very strict with him, refused to let him enter high school and to pursue an interest in scholarly Chinese. They later forced him into a marriage he didn't wish and then, when it proved to be a happy one, forced him and his young wife to separate. After this, he left home for Yokohama, earned some money, learned English from a man educated in America, took passage on an English steamer and arrived in Seattle after seventeen days of travel. That same year, he got a job at the sawmill at Port Blakely.

Hirakawa later recalled his first impressions:

It was supposed to be the largest mill in the State of Washington. Hundreds of workmen were busy in the large room 100 by 300 feet. About 50 men were Americans, 200 were Scandinavians and only 23 were Japanese. They were sailors who had landed from sailing ships... So at Port Blakely I found my second job, to carry lumber and pile it up outside the building; for the ten hours work we received three meals and $1 a day... In the camp of the sawmill there were 24 Japanese living together at the same place... They were working ten hours every day except Sunday, but every night were gambling until midnight or 2 or 3 o'clock in the morning. Therefore, I couldn't sleep by their noisy talking or sometimes with quarrel or fight.

What a start!

Thus one, two, three years sped quickly by, and fortunately

Two story Washington Hotel in Yama on left. Started about 1900 by Hanjiro Kono. Later run by Sohichi Shigemura. Photo courtesy Bainbridge Island Historical Society.

my bad companions went to another place, and they were re-placed by good earnest Japanese farmers, so the environment was much improved. Now no one disturbed my reading or my slumbers. Now I could endure my hard work and enjoy my reading.

Hirakawa stayed at Port Blakely another four years, until he had saved enough money to return to see his family in Japan. Later he would return to America, become an ordained Christian minister, return to Bainbridge Island and found a Japanese mission in Winslow. During World War II he was compelled to leave the island again, returning to it for a third time, in 1947, almost 60 years after his arrival in 1890.

The "camp of the sawmill," about whose noisy residents Hirakawa wrote, was called Nagaya. It was located on the lower slope of the hill southwest of the log pond. A small stream flowed through it, the residents' water source, and that was bridged by a pathway that continued on between the little shacks of the village. It was home for the first bachelor immigrants from Japan.

Hanjiro and Fuji Kono were one of the early Japanese couples to settle in Port Blakely. Hanjiro worked his way across the ocean as a cook and settled in Seattle in 1889. He married Fuji Tanaka in Seattle and the newlyweds moved to Port Blakely. Their home, built with lumber the mill let immigrants use for this purpose, was one of the earliest houses in J-town, as Chiye Shigemura and others often called the place. The land always belonged to the mill company. The Kono house was built a short way up the hill from Nagaya, and that part of J-town became known as Yama.

Hanjiro Kono's son Ralph said his father used to talk about the same men who bothered Hirakawa. Their off-hours gambling games became all-night affairs and impaired their usefulness in the mill as well as the tranquility of Nagaya and nearby Yama. Having the backing of the mill superintendent, Kono was able to put a stop to the gambling and was responsible for the troublemakers moving on. Nagaya's image, and Yama's, too, improved.

Masajiro Furuya was another early Japanese immigrant to Puget Sound who was well known among the Japanese at Port Blakely. He was only twenty-eight when he arrived in 1890, but he joined the Seattle business community right away by opening a small tailor shop. Soon afterward, he began a general merchandising business, M. Furuya Company, and sent salesmen to call on the Japanese people in Port Blakely and other mill towns. To pave the way for his salesmen, he probably called on the Campbells, since they made a point of controlling activities that might compete with the company store. He must have convinced them that he would offer goods only of interest to the Japanese, goods that the immigrants wanted but which the company store could not profitably provide. Thus, his salesmen were welcome. They are remembered as always dressing in the traditional way—in grey suits with black tie.

Furuya also developed a labor brokerage relationship with the mill. That is, his firm would contact Japanese immigrants, tell them of the particular labor needs of the sawmill and of the wages paid (high, certainly, by immigrant standards, but substantially lower than the wages paid to Caucasians) and notify the mill of the labor that was available. Through Furuya's firm, many Japanese newcomers made their first contact with Port Blakely.

The men for whom Furuya found jobs were later called on by his merchandise salesmen. Customers paid for their purchases when they placed their orders and thus helped Furuya finance his business. When the immigrants married, Furuya's sales grew as the families grew. He was an aggressive businessman, and only a few years after starting M. Furuya Company, he had opened branches in Portland, Tacoma, Vancouver, British Columbia, and Yokohama and Kobe, Japan.

Furuya continued to work hard and he developed a staff of dedicated employees. He started a bank for Japanese, Chinese and other Asian immigrants and was its president. Later, he became head of a second bank, and in 1928 he merged the two and became president of Pacific Commercial Bank of Seattle.

As his various businesses prospered, he was able to build a beautiful island summer home and his "Furuya Gardens" at Crystal Springs, about three miles from Port Blakely. The location was almost directly across Port Orchard passage from Captain Renton's second sawmill location at Enetai. The gardens consisted of:

> ...a large greenhouse and eight hot houses on six acres of land stretching 300 feet along the shoreline. We cultivated five thousand pots of lilies, cucumbers, tomatoes, lettuce, geraniums, and chrysanthemums in the fall.
>
> At the time the Furuya Resort House was famous in Seattle's Japanese community. All the trees were shipped from Japan, including many paulownia and maple, and wisteria with white and purple flowers, and there were two lanterns, a pond and a bridge. Thus, the landscape was beautiful. Every Sunday students of the University of Washington and prefectural association people held picnics, but the Furuya employees most enjoyed the advantage of using it.

Those were the Furuya Gardens as remembered by Yoshito Kawachi in the 1970s. He was once Mr. Furuya's property manager.

Unfortunately, Masajiro Furuya's business world came apart during the Great Depression. His Pacific Commerical Bank closed its doors forever on October 24, 1931, and Furuya lost almost everything he had worked for more than forty years to build. So did many others who had counted on him. He moved to California and then to Japan where he died in February, 1938, but his name and the stories of his home have remained a part of Bainbridge Island history.

In the early days of Nagaya, the residents were mostly bachelors. They were called *wataridori*, which means "bird of passage," since they all expected one day to return to Japan.

Many who stayed, however, ended their bachelor days by marrying "picture brides." The marriages were arranged with the help of a *baishakunin*, a go-between in Japan. After an exchange of pictures, each party being satisfied, the young woman in Japan would make the long voyage to Seattle to meet her new husband. There were often surprises. Sometimes they found the man had exaggerated his status or sent pictures taken in younger days. Sometimes they sent pictures of more handsome friends. Still, such marriages often seemed to work out happily.

The Japanese immigrants built Yama along the west slope of the stream that ran down the hill from Jons Petter Peterson's Sunny Hill Dairy. It was a small stream that flowed into the log pond of the mill from the west. Yama wasn't more than a quarter of a mile from the busy sawmill, but it seemed far removed and always had an ambience more Japanese than American.

The houses were built like the rural hillside homes the immigrants had left. They were simple, small, usually unpainted and weathered looking, and almost on top of each other. In time, thick second-growth fir and alder shielded them from the sight of the mill and muffled its sound. It became a sort of Japanese oasis.

The first structure on the stream side of the road, at Yama's lower end, was the Hanjiro Kono's place. After working for a time at the mill, Mr. Kono enlarged the home, and it became the community's two-and-a-half story Washington Hotel. It had a good western style restaurant to which Caucasian mill workers came each day for lunch. The cook, hired by Mr. Kono, was a good baker and his fresh bread was a special attraction. The hotel offered accommodations, meals and Japanese communal baths to visiting salesmen, teachers, doctors and preachers. Up the hill from the hotel a Mr. Ikuta ran the community barber shop.

In 1904, hotel owner Hanjiro Kono sold the Washington

Hotel to Sohichi Takahashi Shigemura, Chiye Umezuka's father.
Mr. Kono moved on to a mill at Campton, near present-day
Redmond. There he again became foreman of the Japanese
workers. Almost simultaneously, Mr. Shigemura, who was still
a Japanese citizen, was called back to Japan to serve in the
army during the Russo-Japanese war. With Mr. Shigemura away
and Mr. Kono off on a new job, Mrs. Kono stayed with Mrs.
Shigemura to run the hotel until its new owner returned.

The children helped, too, of course. Chiye remembers:

> The millworkers toiled from 7 A.M. to 6 P.M. with a one-
> hour break for lunch, six days a week, so their time to enjoy leisure
> was limited. Since we had the restaurant, we worked seven days.
> During school days, we ran home at lunchtime a step ahead of the
> workers to wait on tables, grab a bite and rush back to school on
> time. But it was not all work for us. We had either the *P.I.* or the
> Times, and the Sunday funnies were looked forward to eagerly.

Tamegoro and Tamao Takayoshi operated the next business a few feet upstream. They arrived from Japan in 1898, and in
Port Blakely a story developed that caused some people to address
Tamegoro as "General." His children and grandchildren say that
he never approached that rank in the army, and they have no
idea of where the title came from. However, it suggests the high
regard in which he was held by the people in Yama. To consider
him the village's unofficial mayor would be appropriate.

Tamegoro came from Tsuwano, a lovely mountain village
near the west end of Honshu, the main island of Japan. He and
his wife bought an existing structure overlooking the stream and
developed it into the showplace of Yama. On the side nearest
the Kono's Washington Hotel, they had a grocery store and ice
cream parlor. Upstream from the store was the family home, and
nestled between the home, the store and the road was a patio
covered by wisteria growing on a trellis. Tamegoro put stone lanterns in the patio, and Tamao filled them with flowers, cared for
the vines and plants growing in wickerware pots and made the
patio into a place of beauty. In the summer, tea was served, and
over the years, the Takayoshi's tea garden became well known
far beyond the Japanese community. Later, as man-made ice

Delivery wagon in front of Takayoshi store at Yama. Photo courtesy Puget Sound Maritime Historical Society.

became available, Tamegoro's children helped him make ice cream. They used cream from the Peterson's Sunny Hill Dairy, and a generation of islanders still remember it as the best ice cream they ever tasted. There was even a piano in the ice cream parlor. Young Kimiko Takayoshi played it for dances, with her brother, Tomeo, singing the lyrics to the songs.

Tamegoro must have been Yama's most enterprising citizen. His store had Yama's first telephone. He took orders from people living beyond Yama and delivered to them from his wagon. He had a photography studio and a watch repair shop, and he was also agent for a Seattle laundry company, in competition with Judge Plate. His photographs provide one of the best records of Yama.

Upstream, next to the Takayoshi's, was the Buddhist Temple. It was a spacious building of two stories. In addition to serving as the temple, it served as a school.

Most of the parents in Yama expected, as the *wataridoris* did, that they and their youngsters would someday return to Japan to live. Therefore, it was most important to them that their children be able to speak and understand the Japanese language and know something about the ancestral culture of their parents. The Buddhist temple provided the setting for a school-after-school where their children could be taught. Over the years, several teachers conducted such classes.

In its latter days, Yama was especially fortunate to have arrive in its midst a scholar who had been a teacher and school administrator in Hiroshima. His name was Igi, and he was from a good family in Japan. His parents, like Hirakawa's, had tried to arrange a marriage for him with a girl of their choice, not his, so he decided to emigrate to America. He came to Port Blakely, worked at the sawmill, and lived at the Shigemura's hotel. Before long some of the parents learned of his background in education and persuaded him to become their children's Japanese teacher. His classes were small and they were conducted in family homes. Igi was a "Mr. Chips" kind of a man and quickly won the respect and affection of the children and their parents. When children spoke to him, they used the respectful form of address, calling him Igi-san.

Igi-san took special pains to teach his pupils about Japanese moral and cultural values and the proper way of doing things in Japan. He tried to counter the crude language the youngsters naturally picked up in the milltown. He helped them to better understand their parents' native tongue, and together they put on traditional plays called *shibais*.

Igi-san lived frugally. He was conscious of diet and vitamins and was critical of the children for eating yesterday's equivalent of junk food. He was good at following the foreign exchange market and amassed what seemed a small fortune by investing in it.

In time, Igi-san left Port Blakely and took a job in the railroad roundhouse at Auburn. His sight began to fail him there and he returned to Hiroshima. He survived the war, but was totally blind by its end. A young woman took care of him, but the "small fortune" he made in the foreign exchange market was now exhausted. Hearing of his circumstances, and remembering with affection all that Igi-san had done for their children, several families in Port Blakely sent money to their old friend right up to the time of his death.

Up the hill beyond the Buddhist temple was the community playfield and beyond it the Baptist Mission. A number of the families who came to Yama had become Christians in Japan and some had received help in coming to America from the Baptist Church. In Seattle the First Baptist Church was well established, full of missionary zeal, and desirous of starting missions in the immigrant communities. With the help of that church and particularly of one of its members, Charles Black, and with lumber provided by the mill, the Japanese Baptist Mission in Yama was built and dedicated in 1904. Rev. Fukumatsu Okazaki, of the also recently opened Japanese Baptist Church in Seattle, visited to conduct services.

A trail from the end of the planked road beyond the mission went past Yama's haunted house and on to Pleasant Beach. Pleasant Beach wasn't far away, and the ladies made frequent trips there to get clams and *nori*, the seaweed that grew in the clean waters of Rich Passage. The *nori* was dried over lines strung on the porches at Yama. Once dried, it was heated in ovens until brittle and then crumbled over rice to make one of the healthy and tasty dishes for which it was used.

Tamao Takayoshi and other parents took children from Yama to the beach for summer picnics. A picture survives that was taken at one such picnic. It shows that the children were immaculately dressed, the girls having pretty bows in their hair. Washing clothes and children to have them appear this way for a picnic must have been a chore and a challenge. The picture suggests that this was one of the few ways the young mothers could display the cultural inheritance of tidiness and beauty that they brought with them from their quiet and clean village homes in rural Japan.

Many fathers and most of the boys in Yama found their pleasure in fishing. The boys fished for the perch that fed around the rocks of the millpond dam. When the current was running swiftly in or out of the millpond, the waters could be dangerous. Fathers fished from rowboats for salmon, using homemade lures, pounded out at home from shiny scraps of tin. Ichijo, who worked for the Takayoshis as a cook, had a gasoline launch. He went out almost every day and returned with pails full of rock cod, selling fish to the people of Yama and sometimes even taking fish to Seattle to sell.

Sometimes the whole community would walk the trail

to Pleasant Beach to play games. It was a pretty destination on summer moonlit evenings, too, but you did have to beware of the haunted house when you returned.

The people of Yama got their drinking water from two barrels that were in the creek bottom behind and below the Takayoshi's place. It was the responsibility of the women to carry empty tin containers down to the barrels and bring them home full of clean water. They carried the tins slung from bamboo poles, just as they had done in Japan.

For the women in Yama, there wasn't much need for social organizations. The houses were small; there wasn't much privacy. They talked between the houses and across the hillside paths. The conversation, naturally, was in Japanese, the coarse dialect of the people from Hiroshima contrasting with the softer Yamaguchi and Shimane dialects. The men's jobs necessitated their learning some English, but the women almost never spoke it. It wasn't easy for them to participate in society outside of Yama, although a number of the women did housework for Caucasian families to help with the family income.

Below Yama and in front of Nagaya, on the flat land near the head of the millpond, was a vegetable and flower garden run by the Tamegoro Tsunehara family. It was a neatly tended place that provided abundantly for the greater community. When the Tsuneharas moved back to Japan in about 1920, the land was taken over by the Nagatani family. Mr. Nagatani immigrated in 1914 from a farming village near Kobe. He worked first as a longshoreman at the sawmill and then managed a greenhouse for the Kitayamas at Island Center for three years. In about 1920, the Nagatani family took over the old Tsunehara farm and operated it as a vegetable and strawberry farm until about 1928. Not far from their house was a big old horse barn, later used as a garage by a Mr. Zuber. Mr. Zuber ran a bus service that met the new Port Blakely-Seattle ferry.

Another family that came to Yama was that of Torazo and Kuma Nakao. Through a series of unfortunate episodes, Torazo's father had lost the family estate in the small farming village of Nakamura near Yamaguchi a few miles from Tsuwano. The estate had belonged to the Nakaos for twelve generations, nearly 350 years, and Torazo, the eldest son in his generation, was determined that it should be recovered. At age twenty-six, after a son and daughter had been born to them, Torazo decided that he and Kuma would go to America where opportunities abounded, earn sufficient funds to reacquire the farm and return to Japan. They would leave their two youngsters behind with Torazo's sister until their return.

In 1900, they crossed the Pacific to Tacoma, worked there briefly in a laundry, then moved to Port Blakely, perhaps with the help of Mr. Furuya.

They set up housekeeping in an existing but empty house in Yama. Like the other homes, it was a simple place; rainwater that fell on the tarpaper roofs was saved for bathing and washing.

Torazo went to work for the sawmill and was given the name Harry by his Caucasian co-workers. For a while, he worked in the log pond, where he pushed and sorted floating logs and lined them up to be lifted up on endless chains to the big head-saws—dangerous work, especially for a man who couldn't swim.

Later on, he organized a small crew of Japanese whose job was to make the best use of the waste wood and bark from the mill head-saw that they could. The wood and bark pieces were known as slabs, and before long, Harry Nakao came to be known as Slab Harry.

The slabs were used mainly for boiler fuel on the steam-powered tugs and the steam-powered lumber-loading barges in Port Blakely's harbor. Tugs like the *Favorite* consumed immense amounts of wood; it was piled on their decks and taken to the furnaces as needed. Getting the slabs from the carts, on which the crew hauled them from the mill, to the decks of the boats was a challenge: the decks rose and fell as much as twelve feet with each tide change. The best way, Slab Harry learned, was not to fight nature, so his gang loaded the slabs when the decks of the boats were even with the level of the wharf. This often meant they were loading at times when they would rather have been sleeping.

The men who worked for Slab Harry also hauled wood to homes around the harbor, though men in the Japanese community who were not on Harry's crew would often pick up their own wood supply on their way home. The crew hauled wood to the mill cookhouse and to the hotel. As a result, Slab Harry and his men were well known to most everyone. Toward the end of the mill's days, Harry was the unofficial liaison between the company and the Japanese community. His English wasn't that good, but there was a mutual trust that had developed over the years on both sides.

Through Torazo Nakao's efforts the family home in Nakamura, Japan, was recovered, and it belongs to the family today.

The population in Yama and Nagaya reached a peak of about 200 people living in about fifty houses in the early 1900s. In the years that followed, most of the men who worked in the mill moved on to work in mills in other places. Some, like the Nakaos, stayed on to farm strawberries on the island. Others, like Seinosuke Takayoshi, a brother of Tomegoro Takayoshi, joined with their neighbors to start greenhouse businesses. Seinosuke Takayoshi and Otto Peterson, an immigrant from Sweden and foreman at the mill, went into the greenhouse business on some property on the lower road in New Sweden in 1914. Three green-houses, each 100 feet long by 35 feet wide, were built the next year. They were near the marshy headwaters of Taylor Creek, where Old Mill Road and Taylor Avenue intersect today.

The greenhouses produced cucumbers, tomatoes and other vegetables and flowers. It proved to be exhausting work for everybody. Seinosuke's son, Henry (Sukezo), had the job of loading up a wheelbarrow with boxes of vegetables and pushing it from New Sweden, past the two churches and the school and down the steep hill to the wharf by the company store. Here he would load the boxes onto the *Monticello* for her morning trip to Seattle. In the spring, Easter lilies grew in the greenhouse. They brought $.10 a stem or $.50 a pot and were the family's most profitable product.

Though the town of Port Blakely was in a decline after 1907, there was a flurry of activity at the mill during the First World War, and J-town was not left out. Suddenly, there were photography buffs, a baseball team, amateur actors who put on Japanese variety shows at the Buddhist temple, and communi-ty picnics. Soldiers from FortWard came to have ice cream and dance at the Takayoshi's and to have meals at the Shigemura restaurant. But then it was over.

After the war, the mill closed down. Nagaya became virtually a ghost town, and slowly, the families of Yama left. In the late 1920s, the picturesque community was torn down.

Most of the Japanese who made their way to Port Blakely came because they, like the immigrants who came from Europe before them, had a desire for freedom, for opportunity and, in many cases, for religious tolerance. They brought with them the strengths of their culture. They may not have found all that they expected, but they worked hard, lived with dignity, and did their part in building America.

CHAPTER SEVENTEEN

WEST BLAKELY, NEW SWEDEN, AND THE COUNTRY CLUB: THE SUBURBS AND SOME OF THEIR CITIZENS

Radiating out from the sawmill town was a series of boardwalks that led to its suburbs. The walks cut through the second growth forest, bridged small streams, and crossed fire ponds and swamps to reach the smaller but distinct communities that were out of sight of Port Blakely proper, but only a short distance away. All but one of these communities was a true suburb. The exception related to it hardly at all.

The reader was introduced to Yama in the previous chapter. Another suburb grew up on an eighty-acre tract that Andy P. Anderson platted in 1890. It became known as West Blakely. A year later, John Campbell, on behalf of the mill, acquired land from Michael Thielan (Taylor) and platted the Taylor addition to Port Blakely. It was sold off to individual owners and much of it became known as New Sweden. Toe Jam Hill, Fort Ward, and to a lesser extent Pleasant Beach and Eagledale, were other communities that related to Port Blakely. The Country Club on Restoration Point was the one that hardly related to Port Blakely at all.

Andy Anderson platted his land in West Blakely in five-acre parcels, rather than the one-acre plots of New Sweden. People of Scandinavian heritage were the predominant settlers in both places. The men walked the boardwalks each day to get to work and sometimes returned in the evening with a wheelbarrow of lumber for their new homes. In time, the children who came along used the walks to get to school. Those who remember their school days in Port Blakely say the path from West Blakely led up a slight incline as it headed for town and ran along the edge of a marsh. Footsteps echoed across the marsh and mingled with the calls of birds in the second-growth alder and fir. It was a pretty walk when the weather was dry, but in the winter, the water rose, the boards were often wet, and it was easy to slip or be playfully pushed off into the water. Part of the way, the path paralleled a wagon road, but the road veered away to the north as it descended into town, leaving the boardwalk a narrow cut through the trees.

When West Blakely was first platted, the hillside between Rich Passage and the upper limits of the plat were mostly covered with the tall stumps that remained from the logging of twenty-five years earlier. Most of the new growth was alder, and this was much easier to clear than the huge firs that faced the loggers of the previous generation. There was no use for the alders except for firewood, and the supply went far beyond the newcomers' needs. So the sight and smell of alder smoke from piles of burning waste followed the arrival of every new purchaser of one of Andy Anderson's five-acre tracts.

Each newcomer built a one- or two-room cabin before he cleared his entire tract. There were paths through the woods from one house to another and on the slope and across the flat that ran through the center of West Blakely. Picket fences began to appear to keep in the occasional cow and to keep out the more numerous deer. The deer loved the leaves of the young fruit trees that most every settler planted. The mill made fence pickets by the thousands.

The setting of West Blakely was a pretty one, for the site had a southwest exposure. After the trees were cleared, a number of houses had views of the blue and always-moving waters of Rich Passage and the entrance to Port Orchard. The Miles Cornthwaites could look west across their small pasture and see the southern peaks of the Olympic Mountains. Cornthwaite is remembered as the blacksmith and metal worker who, when not at work at the mill, developed the efficient Cornthwaite wood-fueled heating stove. The top-loaded stove became the center of many Port Blakely-area homes.

The Johannes and Serena Johnson family from Finland moved to West Blakely early, and their daughter, Ida, remembered her father telling her that he and her mother started building their house when they had saved $90. Johnson borrowed a farm wagon to haul his lumber up from the mill. His friends helped with the building; the wives of his friends helped Mrs. Johnson feed the builders.

Frank Nelson, Sr., was another early settler in West Blakely. He came from the island of Oland in Sweden. He and his neighbors formed the Progressive Club of West Blakely and built the first meeting place in the community, a community hall on the hillside near the upper end of today's Lytle Road. There were dances and box socials there, and Martin Peterson, the island's best accordionist, would walk all the way from his home in Eagledale to play for them.

West Blakely's Bethany Lutheran Church was built in 1910 near the waterfront just west of the foot of present day West Blakely Road. A stern Rev. Bangston was its first minister.

The first grocery store to serve the area may have been one opened by Charles Morrill about the turn of the century. When he moved to Winslow to start the pharmacy there with Dr. Kellam, he was succeeded by Mr. Shaw. In 1909 the store was operated by a Mr. Bloomquist, who hired young Charles Lindquist to work for him. Charles and his younger brother, Bert, later bought the store from Mr. Bloomquist. In 1932, the IOOF bought the Progressive Club hall and moved it from up on Lytle Road to West Blakely's main intersection. Charlie and Bert used part of it for their grocery store. In 1934, Clinton R. Cave and Wilbur Nystrom took over the business, and in 1935, they moved the store back across Oddfellows' Road into a new building. Behind the new store was the community baseball diamond.

About this time, Charlie Olson opened a service station on newly-opened Blakely Avenue. During the latter days of the ferry service to Port Blakely, Jim Haggland worked there and he remembers how busy the little hand pump station was just before and after ferry arrival and departure time.

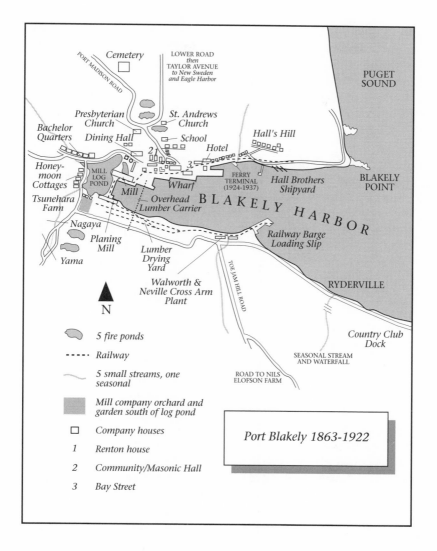

Cemetery

LOWER ROAD
then
TAYLOR AVENUE
*to New Sweden
and Eagle Harbor*

PORT MADISON ROAD

PUGET
SOUND

*Presbyterian
Church*

St. Andrews
Church

*Bachelor
Quarters*   *Dining Hall*

Hall's Hill

School

Hotel

*Honey-
moon
Cottages*

MILL
LOG
POND

2

3

Mill

Wharf

FERRY
TERMINAL
(1924-1937)

*Hall Brothers
Shipyard*

BLAKELY
POINT

*Tsunehara
Farm*

*Overhead
Lumber Carrier*

B L A K E L Y   H A R B O R

Nagaya

*Planing
Mill*

*Lumber
Drying
Yard*

*Railway Barge
Loading Slip*

Yama

TOE JAM HILL ROAD

RYDERVILLE

*Walworth &
Neville Cross Arm
Plant*

▲
N

*Country Club
Dock*

5 fire ponds

- - - - - Railway

SEASONAL STREAM
AND WATERFALL

5 small streams, one
seasonal

ROAD TO NILS
ELOFSON FARM

Mill company orchard and
garden south of log pond

☐   Company houses

1   Renton house

Port Blakely 1863-1922

2   Community/Masonic Hall

3   Bay Street

Not far to the west of West Blakely, George Burchell and
William Lytle operated two saloons, close to the beach that was
once called Sylvan Grove. A resort had been there for a number
of years, but it burned down in 1900; only a few large maple
trees mark the spot. Billy Lytle and his wife Mammie were the
last in business there. When Prohibition closed them down, Billy
started a taxi business and met the boats at Port Blakely.

New Sweden was another distinct suburb, separated from

Port Blakely by the steep hill north of town as well as by fire
ponds and second growth fir. Perhaps because it was a little
closer to the company store in Port Blakely, New Sweden had
no grocery of its own. On John Campbell's 1891 plat of New
Sweden, streets were given names appropriate to a mill-centered
place—Fir, Cedar, Alder, Spruce and Pine—as though substantial
growth was expected. However, only one of those names, Pine
Street, has survived, and it is not located where it was platted.

The two principal roads in New Sweden were called
Upper Road and Lower Road—today's New Sweden and Taylor
Avenues. Otto Peterson built his home on Upper Road. Later
he built several large greenhouses on the flat below his house
on the east side of the headwaters of little Taylor Creek. This is
where Seinosuke Takayoshi and his family first worked after he
left the sawmill.

At a date and for a period of time that I haven't discovered Port Blakely's longshoremen built and met in the
Longshoremen's Hall in New Sweden. It was up the hill and
across Upper Road from Otto Peterson's house. New Sweden
had the virtue of being reasonably close to the wharves in Port
Blakely, and the hall could be built on land not controlled by
the men's employer.

The suburbs were home to many nationalities, not only
the Japanese and Scandinavians but immigrants from other
parts of the world, too. One family that settled in West Blakely
was named Iturri. They came from Arteaga and Guernica in
the Spanish province of Vizcaya near the Bay of Biscay and the
Atlantic Coast border between Spain and France. The Iturris
were Basque and spoke the ancient Basque language as well as
Spanish. Their story is worth recounting.

It is best told by Daniel Iturri, born in Port Blakely in
1920:

> The first member of our family to arrive on the island was
> my Uncle Ignacio, a merchant sailor. That was in 1884, when he
> went to work in the sawmill. He lived in the bachelor quarters at
> first and then had a small house of his own, near Pleasant Beach.
> Uncle Ignacio walked back and forth to the mill each day, and
> when he needed supplies, he pushed a wheelbarrow to town to

help him get them home. Ignacio seemed an odd name to the people he worked with, so they gave him the name Billy Barrow.

My father, Frank Iturri, was Ignacio's younger brother. He left Spain to go to the Philippines, where two other brothers had done well in the import and export business. Father was to be taken in as a partner, but he hated the climate and the country in general and decided to visit brother Ignacio. He arrived in Port Blakely in 1890 and lived with Uncle Ignacio. For several years he worked in the mill and then came the Alaska Gold Rush of 1898. He got the bug and went to Alaska, but returned in 1908, not richer but presumably wiser. At Port Blakely, he became foreman of the lath mill.

In 1910, Dad married my mother, Celeste Basterrechea, by proxy. He had known her in Spain. While Dad had been living his bachelor days, Mother had married, had a daughter and become a widow in Guernica. When Mother got to Seattle, she and Dad were married in a church ceremony there. Then he brought her to the island. Their first home was near the foot of the hill below the Japanese community of Yama.

The Iturris had five children, all boys, and all but one delivered by Dr. Kellam.

Later, we moved to a house in Port Blakely near the road leading past some bachelor cabins up to the community's dam.

Then we moved to a third house, one of the four mill company houses that had once been called the honeymoon houses. They were between the millpond and the Nagatani's farm. Dad paid $9.50 a month to the mill company for the use of it. The house had a nice living room and kitchen, with a large storage room on the first floor and four bedrooms on the second floor. To help their income, Mother and Dad often had a couple of boarders. They were always Basques! By this time, there were the five of us boys and our stepsister, so the house was well filled. We had a large wood stove for cooking and a potbellied stove in the living room for heat in the evenings. No heat in the bedrooms, but plenty of blankets. Our only light was from coal oil lanterns, but we have no recollections of inadequate lighting. There were lots of lanterns. I know, because I had the job of cleaning their chimneys. We bathed in a huge galvanized iron tub in the middle of the kitchen floor every Saturday night—whether we needed a bath or not.

While we were living in the mill houses, Slab Harry delivered firewood to us for $2 a month. When this service was discontinued, Dad would listen for windfalls during storms and after locating the fallen tree, would get permission from Pete Murray, the 'law' in Port Blakely, to cut it up for firewood. We would saw the trunk up into sections 40 inches long and roll each section to our house with the help of an ingenious system of handles nailed to the middle of the ends of each section. We learned this trick from the Filipinos on the island.

Several families picked ferns in the woods and sold them in Seattle. We got crates at the store and picked wild blackberries, shipping them to Seattle, too.

In the early 1920s, the mill was being torn down, and Dad built a barn behind our house with scrap lumber. We had two cows, Pet and Beauty, and some chickens. Pet and Beauty provided more milk than we could use, so we sold the excess to our neighbors.

My brother Anthony died when he was thirteen in a rafting accident on the lake where we got our water. We called it Blakely Lake and passed it often when we went on walks to gather firewood. It was winter when the accident happened, and he was heavily clothed, so he didn't have much of a chance.

We all almost drowned at one time or another. Joe fell off a log raft and was saved by Frank. Frank fell of a log raft and was saved by Joe. Sam went in, bicycle and all, off the Pleasant Beach pier when his bike wheels got stuck in a crack. He was saved by a fellow in a rowboat. I was saved by brother Frank when I fell out of a rowboat in the millpond. I was pretty well gone when Frank pulled me out, but Dr. Kellam brought me back. How we counted on him! We could all dog-paddle, but that was about it. Poor Mother was scared to death for us all the time.

As I said, we had a rowboat in the old millpond and went out through the now unused gates to fish as the high tide ebbed through the old gate. Sometimes we rowed to Blakely Rock and fished there. When the salmon were running, you couldn't tell where you might catch one, but fishing was good off Blakely Point. We loved to dig for clams, and the crabs were beautiful. One time Dad had a horse, and we did some plowing. We rode it, too, but no saddle.

In 1917, my uncle had acquired six still-uncleared acres in West Blakely that were owned by Dr. Kellam. He paid $250 per acre for them. He and my Dad cleared the land of forest and planted fruit trees. Along with the apples, cherries and plums, Dad planted a mulberry tree and a Mediterranean oak, also known as Holm oak. He said the oak was brought to Bainbridge from near his home in Spain. The other trees have disappeared, but the oak grew into a great and beautiful tree and is still there. Uncle Ignacio and Dad then built a barn and a house. For all this, Uncle Ignacio gave Dad a half interest in the place.

Uncle Ignacio became involved in some religious sect and disappeared mysteriously on April 1, 1921. Dad searched communities all over the Sound for him. Finally, in desperation, he decided to search the wells on his six acre West Blakely property once more. Poor Uncle Ignacio was found in one of them. Dad, who buried Ignacio at Port Blakely Cemetary, thinks Uncle Ignacio was murdered by members of the sect for his property.

Dad made his final move on Bainbridge to his and poor Uncle Ignacio's West Blakely property in 1926. That was the year before the school in Port Blakely closed, so while my brothers had started school there, I started at the Pleasant Beach School, where Mrs. Hopkins was the principal. It was just a short walk from home.

On holidays and days of leisure, the Basques would all gather at one or another's home and celebrate with a big meal, then dance and sing. We celebrated weddings in the traditional Basque manner, and we learned to play old-country card games.

We got along well with all the ethnic groups on the island. No problems. As children we were allowed to go to the annual Japanese picnic. They treated us as their own, feeding us rice balls and ice cream. My Dad had Swedish, Japanese and Filipino friends. In general, there was easy mixing and socializing, especially among the younger set.

The Iturri family left Port Blakely in 1929 and moved to

Wilmington, California. Dan and three of his brothers live there now, but how vividly they remember growing up on Bainbridge Island sixty years ago.

As noted at the beginning of this chapter, most of Port Blakely's suburbs depended on the mill town in one way or another, especially for employment. However, in 1891 a rather different community took shape on Gus Sander's farm at nearby Restoration Point. Before this community is described, the reader should be brought up-to-date on the Sanders family, last mentioned when their daughter and her little friend, Mina Elofson, died of scarlet fever.

Gus Sanders celebrated his forty-third birthday in September, 1891. He and his wife Ellen now had four children in their home of sixteen years on Restoration Point. Sanders had been a foreman at the Port Blakely Mill, but then decided to get a job at a mill in Ballard. He was now making still another change—to being a gripman on the Front Street Cable Railway in Seattle. The farm seems never to have interested Sanders enough for him to devote his full energies to it.

In Ballard in 1888, he met a young Norwegian immigrant,

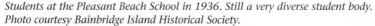

Students at the Pleasant Beach School in 1936. Still a very diverse student body. Photo courtesy Bainbridge Island Historical Society.

Ludvig A. Oien. Oien left Ballard to go to Mora, near the present-day town of LaPush on the Olympic Peninsula. There could hardly have been a more remote spot, but Oien applied for a homestead there and in a few years gained title to it. Before the end of 1891, however, he had had enough of Mora as a permanent home and was back on Puget Sound. He looked up his friend Sanders and took a job with him at Restoration Point, sometimes called Sanders' Point farm.

Clearing was being done near the point to enable Sanders to build a clubhouse for the use of some young businessmen from Seattle. These men were weekend sailors, who found Restoration Point an ideal destination for weekend sailing excursions on their cutter, the *Roxie*.

These recreational sailors were led by E.A. Strout and George A Heilbron. In 1890, Bernard Pelly and W.A. Peters joined Strout and Heilbron in the purchase of a successor to the *Roxie*, the 40-foot schooner *Marjory*, for their excursions to the island. Their continued enjoyment of Restoration Point brought these men and a number of their friends to negotiate with Gus Sanders to buy five and one-half acres of his land right at the tip of the point. On April 16, 1891, the two parties agreed to a purchase price of $1,010.

The clubhouse Sanders, Oien and the others built was a simple but spacious wooden building. The newcomers were all bachelors, and the clubhouse was a place where they could bring their friends from Seattle. Sometimes these friends included young ladies. For the sake of decorum, an iron rod was hung with a curtain, and the men slept on one side, the ladies on the other. A Chinese couple who cooked for the group chaperoned.

In 1892, members of the newly created community, struck by the beauty of the place, agreed to purchase the remaining 103 acres of the Sanders' farm for $22,500. But the next year, 1893, hard times came, and payments to keep the contract debt current couldn't be made. Members of the Country Club of Seattle, as the new community was called, worked out a deal with Sanders whereby they would lease his land for ten years with the option to buy it all at the end of that time for $30,000. Oien, during those years, turned his attention to building up the dairy. Ludvig Oien had turned Gus Sanders' rundown farm back into a successful dairy by 1904 and the dairy continued in operation for many years.

. By 1904 their finances had improved and members of the club were able to exercise their option. When fee title to the property was at last obtained, sixteen building sites were platted, and each member drew a number from a hat to determine which would be his.

The Sanders were generous to Country Club members and shared their water supply with them. Water came from a source above Ryderville, but soon proved inadequate for both the new summer community and the farm. A critical need for water began to be felt just at the time Nils and Fausta Elofson were ready to give up their Mosebake farm. The Country Club purchased the homestead in 1908, two years after the Elofsons moved to West Seattle, and it served as a more than adequate water source through 1999, when the club system was converted to Island Utility Co. lines.

Gus Sanders must not have found being a gripman very rewarding for by 1898 he had moved back into the forest products business and gained sufficient expertise in it to form his own American Lumber and Shingle Company. At last, in 1904, a successful businessman, and with his Restoration Point farm finally sold, he bought a large piece of land on the west side of the fertile Duwamish Valley at Kent. Ludvig Oien followed him there, and the two men developed the Standard Dairy. It was the forerunner of todays Smith Brothers' Dairy Farm. A few years later, Gus Sanders built a spacious and genteel mansion on the west side of the farm. Today, it is one of south King County's most impressive historic landmarks. Tragedy and misfortune marred the years for the Sanders, but Ludvig Oien and his sons became prominent members of the Kent community.

The trip to Seattle from the County Club was a long one, the buggy ride and boat trip via Port Blakely taking the better part of two hours. It was sometimes made awkward for the ladies by the clientele of Mike Lyon's saloon at Ryderville, who shouted not always flattering greetings to passing buggies and horse women. All the men worked in the city and were usually able to spend only weekends and short vacations with their families at the club.

In an effort to improve the situation, a dock was built on the north side of Restoration Point near the west edge of the club property. The steamer *Monticello* began to make stops there in 1907 on its runs between Port Blakely and Seattle. The dock was quite wide and long; a wagon or buggy could be driven to the end of it and turned around. There were two sheds, one for freight and one that provided shelter from the rain and wind for waiting passengers. The water at the end of the dock was deep enough for the *Monticello's* successor, the first auto and passenger ferry to serve Bainbridge island, the *Liberty*. Starting in 1924, the *Liberty* made two or more passenger-only stops at the club each day, on her runs to and from the new auto ferry dock at Port Blakely.

Although they were called cottages in the fashion of New England summer colonies, a number of very fine homes were built in the Country Club. Traditions, quite different from those of the Nordic, Basque and Japanese immigrants were brought west with the early residents. One of these was Saturday tea. The ladies dressed appropriately and were served from a magnificent tea service and offered dainty tea sandwiches. Parents and children attended Sunday night hymns, for which one of the charter members, Mrs. William A. Peters, played the piano. The men played tennis in the rather formal looking fashions of the times and played golf on a nine hole, sand-green course that is said to be the oldest golf links on the shores of Puget Sound.

Not everyone went along with the rather rigid observance of these traditions, however. One resident of several summers, Archibald Clark, finally rebelled at always having to wear knickers or white linen trousers and, in protest, moved to the more informal Wing Point community near Winslow.

૨௬

CHAPTER EIGHTEEN

TURN OF THE CENTURY—
THE OLD ORDER CHANGETH

The years around the turn of the century were years of general prosperity. On December 24, 1900, J.A. Campbell, General Manager, wrote about the mill, "We have the Grinnell Dry Pipe system in our mill and shops, there being about 1500 heads in all. Our mill is 102 ft. wide by 432 feet long, and has two double circulars, three band saws, one gang, three edgers and seven planers. The output is from 275,000 to 300,000 feet per day of ten hours. We have had a portion of the mill running nights most of the time for the past few years, which increases the output to nearly 400,000 feet per day, and employs about 500 men." Conditions were so good that it was hard for the average person in Port Blakely to anticipate that the town might have a bleak future.

When William Cave, Port Blakely's tailor since 1888, became sick toward the end of the century, the town had no difficulty in finding someone to take over his business. Some former residents of Prince Edward Island remembered a good tailor there named John Williams who lived at Crapaud. In 1900, they prevailed on him to become successor to Mr. Cave. John's wife, Mary Anne, soon brought her family across Canada by train to join him. Tailor Williams made clothes in Port Blakely for the next thirty-three years.

John Williams in his tailor shop. Port Blakely Hotel Annex, about 1906. Photo courtesy Daisy Williams Tench, his daughter.

Williams was handicapped by a leg injury suffered years earlier while splitting wood. He limped the rest of his days and at work had to sit on his work table in a most untailorlike fashion, his injured leg over the side of the table, his foot resting on a block of wood. But he could cut and sew with the best of his helpers. Businessmen from Seattle came to Port Blakely to have Tailor Williams outfit them in coats, vests and trousers. Word in the community was that he made boys clothes so well that they sometimes lasted through three brothers.

Business remained good for Hall Brothers Shipyard, too. If there were any problems in the offing for them, it wasn't very apparent, for the yard continued to launch its renowned four-masted schooners at the rate of four a year right on into the new century.

On a different kind of optimistic note, fifty-five-year-old John Campbell, Mill Superintendent, ended his bachelorhood and married Susan Robertson in 1901.

But as if in recognition that all good things must come to an end, a new cemetery was started deep in the woods off the Port Madison Road between New Sweden and Port Blakely school. There is no record of there being a designated community burial ground before the mill company donated the land for this one in 1900. However, there are many monuments in the cemetery that date from prior to this time; so graves must have been moved to the new cemetery from elsewhere.

Wealthy outsiders were entering the local lumber business. It was learned that R.L. McCormick, a millionaire lumberman from Wisconsin, was interested in acquiring the vast acreage of timberlands that the Northern Pacific Railroad had received for constructing its transcontinental line to Tacoma. Successful as the owners of the Port Blakely Mill Company were, their resources were far less than those of a number of Midwesterners. In the industry, it was well known that Wisconsin and Minnesota, as well as Michigan, were so completely cut over that the timber barons there had to move on if they expected to stay in the business. And they were looking toward the West Coast. In the late summer of 1899, it was the Weyerhaeuser syndicate, not R.L. McCormick, which paid $6 an acre to acquire more than one million acres of Northern Pacific timber, mostly in Washington State.

Three years later Weyerhaeuser announced it would erect several large mills in the state and construct logging railroads from the new mills to the timber belt, as they referred to the Northern Pacific timber. The company was to operate all its own logging camps and railroads and planned to "engage in the lumber business on an extensive scale," according to a newspaper of the time. Timbers for the eastern market, which were in large demand, were to be the specialty of the mills. The general opinion was that the new firm would invade the cargo as well as the rail trade. Though it later turned out that they were merely whistling in the dark, some well-posted lumbermen boasted that the coming of this vast new enterprise would not in any way affect local conditions.

A rumor began that the Port Blakely Mill Company was to be sold. The rumor was that the purchaser would be the Southern Pacific Railroad. During the winter of 1902, the management of the mill acknowledged that negotiations for a sale had been in progress for some time. Charles S. Holmes, mill company president in San Francisco, suggested that there might be other interested buyers. "The mills are for sale if anybody will offer our price, but nobody has offered it yet," he told reporters.

Several years before his death, Renton and Holmes had entered into an agreement that in the event of the death of either, the other would carry on the business for ten additional years to provide against a weakening of the business by division. It was just over ten years since Captain Renton's death, and Holmes had fulfilled his commitment to the mill's founder. He not only kept his end of the bargain, but also realized that the time had come to sell.

Holmes was now seventy years old and Campbell was a newly-married fifty-six and that might have entered into their thinking, too. There were no likely management successors, forty-nine-year-old Assistant Superintendent James Campbell not wishing the job. It is possible that the unusually severe forest fires of 1902 that so threatened their Mason County timberlands and equipment may also have influenced them.

Furthermore, the estates of Captain Renton and R.K. Ham were represented among the stockholders, and Holmes and Campbell could not cash them out without assuming an unacceptable level of debt or selling the company.

Holmes and Campbell must have felt a reluctance to sell the mill to which they had devoted their business careers, but they at least could take some comfort in the fact that they were entertaining offers on a strong market.

In January, 1903, a group did offer the right price. From San Francisco, Holmes announced that he and his associates had sold their interests in the Port Blakely Mill Company to a group of Michigan and San Francisco capitalists, not to the Southern Pacific Railroad.

The driving forces behind the buying group were David Edward Skinner and John W. Eddy, both recently of Bay City, Michigan, where their interests had been in the lumber and associated salt businesses. Skinner was named president of the company with an office in San Francisco, and Eddy, several years younger than Skinner, became general manager in Port Blakely.

David Edward Skinner. Photo courtesy Skinner family.

John W. Eddy. Photo courtesy Garret Eddy.

T.C. Ford, born in Ireland in 1850, became the superintendent of the mill.

While Holmes and Campbell may have felt they saw economically threatening handwriting on the wall, the buyers clearly felt they'd made a wise purchase. They were experienced lumbermen; they knew the markets; and they had acquired a going concern.

At the time of the sale, Holmes was managing a number of his own investments in San Francisco, mostly real estate, in addition to the affairs of the mill company. After the sale, he and his two sons created the Holmes Investment Company, with its offices in the Foxcroft Building in San Francisco, a building the family owned. Renton's longtime key associate, Holmes, the man who ran the enterprise for the twelve years after Renton's death, died on December 24, 1906, three years after the sale. In April of that year, the disastrous San Francisco earthquake and fire destroyed the company's San Francisco retail yard, its offices and all the mill company records stored there.

John Campbell left Port Blakely and acquired a mill at Campton near Redmond at the north end of Lake Sammamish. Many of the mill workers went with him, including Hanjiro Kono, who, as noted earlier, again became foreman of the Japanese workers.

It was the intent of the new owners to continue and probably to modernize the fifteen-year-old mill. The business people in the community must have welcomed this prospect of offsetting the reality of Hall Brothers Shipyard carrying out their plan to move the yard to Madrone on the north side of Eagle Harbor. "Five-masted schooners like the *Inca* and the *George E. Billings*," Henry Knox Hall said of the move, "were the largest that could be built at the Port Blakely yard." To remain in business, the company had to be able to build larger ships, mostly steamships. Furthermore, a better ship-repair facility was needed, and a dry dock could not be built in the already crowded Port Blakely site.

Neither was a location beside a large sawmill any longer key to the success of a shipyard as it had been in 1880. More and more ships were being built of steel. Larger storage areas were needed, and steel could be shipped to Eagle Harbor as easily as to Port Blakely. Steel ships were heavier than the wooden ones, and new ship ways needed to be built.

At the time of the 1903 move to Eagle Harbor, where a far more suitable shipyard site was available, Henry Knox Hall was seventy-seven years old. His son, James Hall, took over as manager at the new yard. James had learned the business from the bottom up, apprenticing at Port Blakely in the mold loft at the age of twenty-four. Madrone's citizens were so pleased to have the shipyard move to their townsite that they even changed the name of the community to Winslow, honoring Winslow Hall who had designed the firm's famous lumber schooners as well as its other ships.

The move had a serious impact on Port Blakely. For twenty-three years, the shipyard had employed between fifty and one-hundred people. Those people traded at the store, patronized the bar and the dining room at the Bainbridge Hotel, had haircuts from Judge Plate and were brought back to good health after accidents or sicknesses by Dr. Kellam. They were members of Port Blakely's fraternal organizations, and they rode the *Sarah M. Renton* to Seattle and back. The well-kept Hall mansion up on Hall's Hill would now fall into other hands, hands probably less able to afford to care for it, and its gardens and tennis courts, than the Halls had been. The shipyard would continue,

Port Blakely Presbyterian Church, about 1910.

first under John MacAteer and then as a maintenance yard and winter moorage for sailing ships and auxiliary vessels of the Northwestern Fisheries Company. But a premier employer was lost, and this was a blow to everyone in Port Blakely as well as to the town's image and its ego.

At this time, the last two ships the Hall Brothers would build at Port Blakely were on the ways. They were the company's Hull Numbers 108 and 109, the seventy-seventh and seventy-eighth of its ships to be built on the harbor. One was the gasoline launch *Klatawa*, and one was a five-masted schooner. The schooner was to carry the name of Winslow Hall's successor in San Francisco and be christened *George E Billings*, a ship whose fast sailing times and profitable voyages would perpetuate the name of its builders for many years.

Communities sometimes seem to have the attributes of people. One of those attributes is the instinct for survival. In spite of the blow of the shipyard's move, the people of Port Blakely took on a major project to show the world that their town was not only alive and well, but also moving forward. They decided that a church should be built.

Up to this point, Port Blakely church services had been held in homes or in the Masonic Hall. Even though business directories made reference to churches, there is no evidence that a church building ever existed in Port Blakely until 1905. In 1904, Effie McConnell held a meeting of the ladies of Port Blakely at her house, and there the idea for the church really took form. The ladies assumed the job of raising money for it and held a number of bazaars and benefits. They persuaded John Eddy to have the mill company donate the building site, a lot at the top of the Port Madison Road hill, and then to give a substantial discount on the building material. The dedication took place on March 19, 1905, less than a year after the first meeting at Effie McConnell's. The church was always known as the Port Blakely Presbyterian Church.

While the building that housed the church has long since gone, copies of the *Port Blakely Cook Book*, "arranged" by the Ladies Auxiliary of the church, still survive. The date of its publication isn't recorded, and there is no recipe by Effie McConnell or any of the other ladies whose names were placed in the church cornerstone when it was laid, so the book probably is of a later date. But in it are the names and favorite recipes (including Jessie Kellam's recipe for suet pudding) of some ladies who worked to keep the church going. The ladies twisted the arms of local people for ads and listed are Judge C.A. Plate, "barber and agent for the Berlin Dye Works of Seattle"; the Northwestern Fisheries Company; the Store Department of the Port Blakely Mill Company; Carlson Brothers (C.J. and A.W. Carlson, operators of a marine ways on the south side of the Harbor—the yard was bought by Finnish boat builder J.C. Johnson in 1918, and operated by him until 1928); C.C. Kellam, M.D.; T. Takayoshi, "American and Japanese Merchandise, Photographer, Laundry Office, Agent of Watchmaker," and a number of others.

The same year the church opened, Port Blakely was visited by the full-rigged British ship *Wanderer*. On board was twenty-seven-year-old John Masefield, who later became poet laureate of England. He wrote a book called The Wanderer and a poem called "A Mainsail Haul" about his voyage. What he wrote about the mill and the town was no more lyric or poetic than what Seattle newspaper reporters had written. But his story added an Englishman's observation to those of the reporters. He concluded his account by saying that the Wanderer's lumber cargo from Port Blakely "is still remembered in Liverpool as the finest consignment of choice timber ever brought to the port."

In 1905, the sixteen-year-old *Sarah M. Renton* was taken off the Port Blakely-Seattle run and replaced by the newer and somewhat more commodious steamer *Dix*. Like some of the other Mosquito fleet steamers that provided transportation on the Sound, the *Dix* operated with only a captain, a mate and an engineer. The captain would take the boat into the pier in Seattle, unload his passengers, load passengers for Bainbridge and then back the steamer away from the wharf, turn her around and get her headed for the island. Then, he would turn the helm over to the mate and go below to collect fares from the passengers.

On the return trip to Port Blakely Sunday evening, November 18, 1906, Captain Percy Lerner was below collecting fares, leaving a new mate in the pilothouse. It was a pleasant, clear night, not much activity on the Sound. The steam schooner, *Jeanie,* was approaching from Smith Cove on her way to Tacoma. One vessel needed to alter course, and the rules of the road required that to be the faster more maneuverable *Dix*. For some reason that Captain Lerner could never fathom, his new mate, instead of slowing or veering away from the approaching *Jeanie*, turned right across her bow, panicked and held his new course. The *Dix* was struck amidships from her starboard side and sank stern first within minutes. There was no time for most of those in the cabins to escape, and those on the tilting deck were thrown into the water by the impact. The *Jeanie* put out rescue boats, but of the seventy-seven people believed to have been on board the *Dix*, forty-five are thought to have drowned.

Nearly all of the *Dix's* passengers were residents of Port Blakely, and almost every family in the town lost a member or a friend. The son of postmaster Harry Price died a hero when he helped save thirteen-year-old Alice Simpson, the only female to survive the wreck. Roland Price and John McBain managed to get Simpson out of the cabin onto the deck, from which they were all washed overboard. McBain and Price then took turns holding Simpson up. McBain lost his hold on her and floated away, but was later rescued. Simpson's skirts helped keep her afloat in the icy water, and she begged Price to leave her and swim to the *Jeanie* to save himself. But he wouldn't go, and when the *Jeanie's* boat picked up Simpson, Price had disappeared. At 11 P.M., after nearly four hours of searching for survivors, the *Jeanie* returned to Seattle with those her crew had rescued.

A planer at the mill, James A. Jones, later recounted a frightening story of his unsuccessful attempt to save a woman while the two floated in the water. The woman let go of him when a wave hit them, and Jones "turned just in time to see her upraised hand disappear."

Lanesia Anastasia Ford, wife of the mill superintendent, T.C. Ford, was lost in the accident as were the manager of the Port Blakely store, C. Buyler, and his brother. Captain Lerner was saved and had his own harrowing story of being plunged into the water and then rescued. He never skippered a passenger vessel again.

Steamer <u>Monticello</u>. *Photo courtesy University of Washington, Special Collections, UW3910.*

Residents of Port Blakely crowded the landing when the *Florence K.* brought the survivors over from Seattle early the next morning. No one knew which friends or relatives had drowned and which had survived until the steamer unloaded. A reporter present commented that a walk through the streets of Port Blakely that night meant the "running of a gauntlet of shrieks and moans of grief stricken wives and mothers..." The mill was closed on Monday and Tuesday out of respect for the dead. Flags on sailing ships and steamers and at the school, post office, store and hotel were flown at half mast. Black crepe paper was hung over many doorways.

Most of the bodies of those drowned were never recovered, so for many years their final resting place was unmarked. Sixty years after the disaster a memorial plaque recalling it was placed in a park near Alki Point. In the cemetery at Port Blakely there is a large obelisk dedicated to the memory of the five members of Port Blakely's Knights of Pythias Lodge who went down on the *Dix*.

Numbed by what had occurred, people at Port Blakely slowly resumed their lives. The steamer *Monticello* took over the Port Blakely-Seattle run, and her new schedule replaced that of the *Dix* on the chalkboard mounted on the wall between the entrance to the post office and Candy Johnny's cigar, candy and news shop on the wharf.

ॐ

CHAPTER NINETEEN

DISASTER, 1907 STYLE, AND THE AFTERMATH

At night, whatever wind there is on the harbor drops to nearly a calm. That is one of the delights of Port Blakely.

In the last days of the great mill, arriving on such an evening was special. The bow of the *Monticello* cut smoothly through the dark water, the quiet pulse of its steam engine about to be silenced for the last few hundred feet into the wharf. Night lights were on at the MacAteer Shipyard and twinkling at the houses up on Hall's Hill, still called that despite the absence of the Halls. In fact, the whole north shore was lighted up, from the Williams' house nearest Blakely Point to the brightly lighted mill, where the second shift was at work.

With the conversion of the south side of the harbor to drying yards, the crossarm plant and the railroad barge slip, it was much darker there than it had been when houses were spread along it. Only at Ryderville could a little cluster of lights be seen off the port side of the entering steamer. Hardly visible were the stacks of drying lumber that stretched from close to the crossarm plant all the way to the Tsunehara's farm.

The night of April 22, 1907, was just such a quiet night. What little breeze there was, was blowing onshore from the harbor, but hardly rippling the surface. The mill company's four-masted schooner *Blakely* was tied up at the lumber-loading wharf, "stern to," and eleven other ships were in the harbor, three of them large barks, one the British *Balmoral*.

The mill noise, seemingly muffled by the night, suggested that good times had returned to the harbor. The sounds of heavy log carriages trundling back and forth, of dozens of saws, of whistles and steam was the perfect music to lull day-shift workers and their families to sleep. Nor did the light in the sky from the huge waste burner keep the residents awake. They were all used to the bright orange glow that the burner cast on the clouds.

But at 11 P.M., tranquility turned into awesome calamity. Just as had happened eighteen years earlier, a journal box overheated, and caused a fire to start, almost explosively, in the planer room adjoining the main building of the mill. Although the mill was supposedly protected by its costly sprinkler system, supplemented by a network of fire hoses, the fire spread so quickly to all parts of the mill that the men on the night shift had no opportunity to use the hoses, and the sprinklers proved incapable of containing the flames.

In the absence of John Eddy, who was in Seattle, T.C. Ford, resident manager, took personal charge of the volunteer fire fighters. Hydrants and hoses were used to wet surrounding buildings, warehouses and nearby homes. After receiving a call from Port Blakely's postmaster, Harry Thomas Price, Seattle sent its fire boat, the *Snoqualmie*, to the scene of the fire. While she didn't arrive until the blaze was nearly over, the *Snoqualmie* was given credit for saving the adjoining buildings, her two-inch streams of water being far more effective than the volunteer equipment. Once more, a newspaper reporter left the most complete record:

> The *Monticello*, tied up for the night, was hastily brought back into service and maneuvered so that her hoses could be turned on some of the ships and piles of lumber. Fortunately, there was not much lumber stock on the wharf. Only the schooner *Blakely* suffered some slight damage to her stern. The valuable

machine shop, lying less than 100 feet from the main structure of the mill, was in serious danger several times, but volunteer firemen saved it from damage.

Before it became clear that the fire was being contained to the docks and would not spread to the rest of the community, every house was thrown into excitement. Women hastily threw household things together so they might flee with their most precious items. Later, when it was clear that they wouldn't have to flee, they gathered into little knots and gave themselves over to the fascination of the spectacle. Postmaster Price's wife, when interviewed later, told of the wide illumination that the burning mill cast into the night and how children clung to their mothers' skirts out of sheer fright. All the heavens, she said, were crimson, and men working hundreds of feet away on the docks could be seen with distinctness.

The destruction of one of the largest lumber manufacturing institutions in the world took less than one hour.

Late on the day following the fire, John Eddy made the following statement for the press:

> The Port Blakely Mill will be rebuilt. About 50 percent of the plant was destroyed. The loss is about $300,000 and the insurance $200,000, distributed among a number of companies. The work of clearing up the ruins will begin at once. We need all the men we can get, and I believe that all the mill crew who wish it will find plenty of work.

This time, the future wasn't as clear as it had been after the fire in February of 1888. Then the market was strong, and the Port Blakely Mill held a commanding position in it. Now conditions had changed, largely because of the completion of the transcontinental railroads and the construction of miles of branch lines that opened up vast new sources of timber. The number of sawmills capable of turning out twenty million board feet of lumber a year had doubled between 1900 and 1905. In 1906, there were 923 sawmills operating in Washington State. They were widely scattered, and most were small, but their combined output was enormous. At the same time, the growing demand for lumber in the traditional markets had leveled off. The long period of recovery after the collapse of 1893 came to an end with the nationwide economic panic of 1907. The lumber market began a decline that, as one industry magazine estimated, forced the closure of seventy percent of the sawmills in the Pacific Northwest by the end of 1908. Port Blakely, which had experienced annual production of 120 million board feet as recently as 1906, suffered along with all the other sawmill communities.

As if the fire and the intense competition weren't enough to give John Eddy and David Skinner grave concern, insurance adjustors added to their problems. After picking over the debris from the fire and talking to everyone who would talk to them about just what had happened, the adjustor argued that the sprinkler system was incorrectly located and hadn't been tested as it should have been. Instead of giving the mill owners a check to cover the loss, the insurance carriers claimed they weren't liable. This was preposterous, said the owners. For years, premiums had been paid and accepted by the insurance carriers. The insurance map detailing every aspect of the installation had been made the summer the sprinkler system was installed, and there was no record of dissatisfaction with the design or

The third mill. Photo courtesy Bainbridge Island Historical Society.

maintenance of the system in the numerous insurance inspections made since then.

The claim was settled eventually in the courts, which ruled in favor of the mill company. The mill was rebuilt, but partly because of the suit and partly because of the sluggish markets, it didn't start operating until August, 1909, nearly two and a half years after the fire. It was rebuilt as a single mill, in contrast to the double mill that had burned, with a capacity of 300,000 board feet of lumber a day, substantially less than the 400,000-board-foot capacity of the great mill. The new mill incorporated a lath mill, five planing machines, a large dry kiln, and an auxiliary mill for smaller sizes of lumber.

In a concrete fireproof building that still stands, a huge 800-horsepower steam engine drove the main shaft, which extended the entire length of the mill building. This shaft powered much of the mill machinery.

Electricity was generated in the same concrete engine room by two dynamos, one a 300-kilowatt generator driven by a 500-horsepower steam engine. Besides power for the auxiliary mill, it and a smaller generator furnished power for the planing mill and equipment in the machine shop and the foundry. They also furnished electricity to light the plant. Steam for these generators and engines was furnished by boilers located just about where the ones had been in the old mill.

One innovation in the new mill was an aerial cableway used to carry sling loads of green lumber from the mill to the dry kiln across the harbor.

Victor Hugo Elfendahl was hired as assistant general manager to work with Mr. Eddy and Mr. Ford in the management of this finally completed third mill. Experienced in marketing lumber, he had begun work in San Francisco lumberyards at the age of thirteen. He later worked for subsidiaries of the Port Blakely Mill Company, and in 1907 was sent to New York as manager of one such subsidiary, the Douglas Fir Lumber Company. In New York, he opened up a new market for the mill when he persuaded contractors building one of the city's elevated railways to use its timbers.

In spite of Elfendahl's marketing skill, the new mill did not run to capacity during the first few years. The market just wasn't there for all the lumber the industry was capable of producing. The mill struggled to make a profit and did so through 1912. It operated only spasmodically in 1913 and 1914 and lost money both years.

While there were these pessimistic business signs, some citizens of Port Blakely were optimistic, or perhaps it was something else that caused the Roman Catholics in town to think about building a church. They had met for the previous four years in the home of one of the mill machinists, a Mr. McLaughlin, with visiting priest, Father Winters, conducting Mass at a number of these services. In 1914, Mrs. Patrick Fox and Mrs. Charles McDonald, along with some other ladies, collected enough funds to undertake to build what became St. Andrew's Catholic Church. They chose a location across the fire pond above the public school, and the mill company gave them a fifteen-year lease on the site. Mill manager Elfendahl gave them a discount on the cost of lumber.

To get enough money for an organ, the ladies sponsored a dance in the Masonic Hall. It netted them $60, but the organ they wanted was to cost them $70. Hearing of their disappointment, Elfendahl found an extra $10 for their fund. Andrew Towey, who worked at Creosote, was the sexton. He and his wife, Annie, had emigrated from Ireland. Andrew walked from their home in Eagledale to St. Andrew's to care for his church.

St. Andrew's Catholic Church at Port Blakely.

If the ladies were motivated by optimism, their optimism was misplaced, for in 1914, while the church was completed, the mill ceased to operate. If they were motivated by a fear that the peace of the world was about to be shattered, they were right. The world was at war by late summer.

Governments commandeered steamships and that brought about the return to service of retired sailing ships. The mill company created the Port Blakely Transportation Company in 1915 to acquire five ships of the defunct Globe Navigation Company. Charter rates became so attractive that Elfendahl purchased the one time sailing ship, but now a barge, *Gardiner City*, and converted her back into a sailing ship, a barkentine that was christened the *Kitsap*. The mill began operating again and the *Kitsap* sailed in the fall of 1915 with a full cargo of Port Blakely lumber for Honolulu. It was like old times!

Victor Elfendahl succeeded T.C. Ford as General Manager and handled the operating affairs of both the sawmill and the transportation company. D.E. Skinner and John Eddy turned their attention to shipbuilding. They saw greater opportunities there than in the lumber business, so in 1916 leased the sawmill to the Dominion Mill Company and started the shipbuilding firm of Skinner and Eddy. They brought Elfendahl to Seattle as assistant to Mr. Skinner.

Getting old—no longer the mill Captain Renton knew. The third mill in about 1918. Photo courtesy University of Washington, Special Collections, Curtis 17859.

At Port Blakely the Dominion Mill Company called back as many former employees as it could contact. Most of the former Japanese workers returned, often to the same houses they had lived in before. There was a great reunion and renewed hope for the town.

The Skinner and Eddy Corporation was enormously successful in its new enterprise and set many production records. But when the war was over, the market for new ships collapsed as quickly as it had mushroomed only four years earlier. The market for lumber did the same thing, and three years before its lease terminated, the Dominion Mill Company returned the mill company to its owner. In 1919, Mr. Skinner and Mr. Eddy created a new Skinner and Eddy Corporation which became a holding company for the shipyard and the mill. But less than six months later, in June of 1920, Mr. Skinner announced the demolition of the shipyard facilities.

While 1920 was a poor year in the lumber business, 1921 was better and 1922 promised to be better still. Victor Elfendahl returned as General Manager of the sawmill, and his opinion agreed with those who felt low-cost water transportation made fir to New York competitive with pine shipped there from the south. The foreign situation was largely dominated by Japan, he said, and the market there was firm. Others thought the markets in Europe and South America would improve.

Elfendahl brought his family back to Port Blakely and they set up housekeeping in a large home that had been built on the site of the old home of Captain Renton. He felt expansive enough about the future to decide to do what Dr. Kellam, Mr. Otto Peterson, Mr. Furuya and others had done and go into the greenhouse business. The location for this venture of his was on the side of the hill east of the marsh at the head of Pleasant Beach. It was across the marsh from the greenhouses built by Dr. Kellam, and above those operated by Takeshi Kitayama for Emmanuel Olsen.

But for Port Blakely, the perceived opportunities for continued profitable operation of the sawmill proved to lack substance. Work at the mill was so slow that a number of the carpenters there were glad to be employed by Mr. Elfendahl to build his greenhouses. He then employed Kiochi (Frank) Furuta to run them. Furuta emigrated from Hiroshima, Japan, in about 1906. He worked first in Seattle at a restaurant with his brother who had preceded him. Then, when Port Blakely's third mill got underway, he found a job in the planing mill. In 1920 he left the mill to run Mr. Elfendahl's greenhouses. Later he rented the property and continued there for a total of 21 years.

As Mr. Skinner saw it, the lumber business was one with which he no longer wished to be associated. Mr. Eddy shared this view, at least as far as the operation of the sawmill at Port Blakely went. The sawmill was closed down in 1922 and from his office in Seattle Mr. Eddy announced that milling would not be resumed. In 1923, Mr. Skinner and Mr. Eddy separated their financial interests and Mr. Eddy became the owner of the now defunct mill at Port Blakely as well as the valuable timberlands the company still owned, on Bainbridge Island, in Mason County and elsewhere. Mr. Skinner formed the Alaska Steamship Company.

Dismantling of the mill at Port Blakely was undertaken in 1924.

CHAPTER TWENTY

EBB TIDE: THE YEARS REMEMBERED

When the tide is high in Blakely Harbor, it sometimes reaches up into the driftwood and starts it floating. On the beach at Port Blakely on such a day, old-timers ponder about the driftwood, recalling how much there used to be and how little there is today. They shake their heads and wonder where all the driftwood went that was left behind from mill days.

As their talk floats along, the stories stack up much as the driftwood once did. Those who tend to brag argue that the Port Blakely of the early 1900s had the best baseball team on the island. Others remember going to "picture shows" on Friday nights at the old Please You Theatre.

The days after the 1907 fire, when the mill company was operating in fits and starts, were lean ones for most of the residents of Port Blakely. A few years before he died in 1977, Alfred Johnson described those difficult days long before "the Depression," in a talk before the Bainbridge Island Historical Society. He remembered Martin Howley, who had an old horse and a small dairy farm, who delivered milk in the morning, "a tin quart measure, six cents a quart and I'll just give you a little extra because the kids could use it, I guess," Johnson remembered.

Scrounging for food, Johnson and other youngsters went

to the mill company cookhouse where Ching Hing, the Chinese cook, would always say, "Get out of here, you damn kids," and then pass them a piece of cake at the same time.

Then there was old man Ludvig that ran the butcher shop. They all growled at us, but most of them gave. They understood. Give you two and three weiners—Get out of here, get out—he had the baloney all hanging down there and he picked up a knife and he slabbed down on them, and the slab itself would be about that thick, and I'm not kidding. He'd give you a big hunk of baloney cut on the bias. Get out. So we'd get out when we'd get the baloney.

Henry Larson, whose father had run the mill company's retail lumber yard, remembered that one of the main figures in those waning days of the mill town was Pete Murray who was the law in Port Blakely. He had the right to throw someone in "the 10 by 10," as the jail was called. The "10 by 10" was a brick building measuring ten feet by ten feet, with two windows with bars on them in the four-inch-thick walls.

Murray's job was dangerous, and like any lawman, he made enemies. One time he found a man's body in the millpond and later caught the murderer at Fletcher Bay. He asked the murderer why he killed the man and was told, 'I didn't mean to. I was laying for you.'

Alfred Johnson recalled Murray, too.

Murray gave Port Blakely kids good reason to toe the line. If we pulled capers at nighttime, he'd pull up two of us, one under each arm, walk up the street and put that one inside that fence and the next one inside the next fence and say, 'If I catch you out again, I'll throw you in the 10 by 10.' And we'd see guys that he took to that 10 by 10. Absolutely dark, dirt floor, and when they'd come out they didn't want any more of it. So all he'd have to do to us kids was holler '10 by 10' and we were gone.

Murray had a booming voice, though memory has it that

he was basically softhearted and saved more than one would-be criminal from the harder hand of the county law.

Baseball teams provided much of the entertainment around the island, and Johnson—and many other old-timers— swore the Port Blakely team was the best. The mill company put up the money for baseball gear. The team played at first at Pleasant Beach and then moved to a field on the south side of Blakely Harbor near the foot of Toe Jam Hill. Johnson said:

> The money that changed hands betting there on a Sunday was something. The whole island went over there to watch those guys play. And they were ball players. I mean you didn't hang on on that team. You either give or get out. It was sort of a semi-pro team, and this way some of them get $3.50 a game, some get $5.

Admission was charged for the games, and Freda Adams of Toe Jam Hill and Ryderville remembered some youngsters played their own game of running in under the bleachers to get in free when attendants' backs were turned. The grandstands held several hundred people, and there was an ice cream stand for refreshments. A brass band of about twenty musicians played in between innings and before and after the game. A few of the Port Blakely players went on to the pros, giving their fans at home yet one more reason to brag.

The "Please You Theatre" was what the Masonic Hall became when it wasn't being used for lodge meetings, a church meeting, a dance, or some other function. George Beck was the impresario. As in most theaters of the period, the stage curtain had a scene painted on it. There was a painted window in the scene and a hole right through the window. If you were backstage, you could look out the hole and count the audience. Road shows would come along and put on acts, "westerns and a bunch of stuff like that, with cap pistols poppin' off and everybody's clapping," Johnson said.

> Those days as seldom as you'd see a show, you'd start applauding when you started walking into the theatre. From there it went to motion pictures; that is, a man would come over with a mo-

tion picture machine and nine times out of ten those films were all worn out when he got there. The thing that I remember most is not the pictures, but, 'One moment please, the operator's in trouble,' or something like that. Seen that more than anything else.

Entertainment for the "New Sweden gang," a bunch of youngsters who lived up on the hill, meant harassing other kids. Johnson remembered the "rousing welcome" he and his young brothers got as they headed down the boardwalk from New Sweden to the mill just after noon one day. Morning classes had just finished. The New Sweden gang came running out, grabbed the Johnsons' wheelbarrow and other garden gear and tossed it into the pond between the school and St. Andrews Church. "They laughed and went on. We fished it all out and got goin' through a back trail to Hall's Hill."

Later, about 1911, the Northwestern Fisheries fleet, including several barges, took over the site of the old shipyard below Hall's Hill. On Saturdays, when the fleet was in, the kids would use the decks of the barges for a skating rink and roller skate all day.

Across the harbor lived the "grounded adventurers," as Freda Adams called them. They were sailors who had jumped ship to make Port Blakely their retirement home. Freda lived in Ryderville. There was a waterfall in her backyard where a stream tumbled down the bluff from what had been the Elofson's farm up at Mosebake. Her home was small, simple, and tranquil, a far cry from what it must have been in Ryderville's more boisterous days. Freda delivered newspapers to a number of these grounded adventurers who lived across another stream that ran down Toe Jam Hill from the back slope of Mosebake. She remembered them well: Charlie Watson, Handsome Harry, John Bean (possibly a distant relative of Reuben?), Big Mouth Nels, and Winnipeg Charlie.

Toe Jam Hill is a name that astonishes some people, offends others, and puzzles many, but one about which most old timers are very defensive. One time a would-be developer tried to change the name to Blakely Heights, but that name faded and Toe Jam Hill stuck. Freda said there were about as many stories about how Toe Jam Hill got its name as there were story tellers.

Hank Larson remembers catching three or four salmon a night when fishing off the old log-booms in the harbor. He tells of walking through the dark on the boardwalk to West Blakely, whistling all the way so he wouldn't come upon another walker unexpectedly. And he remembers hearing the old pump organ in the Presbyterian church when Mr. Preston, the Sunday organist, would fuel up on hard cider and sneak into the church for a private concert.

As in most harbor towns, a fair amount of bootlegging went on in Port Blakely during Prohibition. Bootleggers loaded their boats there and had a few customers in town. One, according to Alfred Johnson's reminiscences was Tailor Williams, who bought liquor for his own "pleasure and benefit." A few men with absolutely no interest in a new suit of clothes made regular stops at Tailor Williams' shop.

In 1917, when the third sawmill was briefly revived under the Dominion Mill Company, the harbor seemed something like its old self. But just a year later, the telegraph crossarm factory closed. There were fewer employees in the sawmill, so some of the old bunkhouses along the hillside at the north edge of the road to West Blakely were torn down.

In 1920, the grocery store on the dock was closed and moved to the now quite rundown Bainbridge Hotel, still operated by Fred Ziegler, a resident of Port Blakely since 1888. The grocery was operated by Charles Nelson and Jack Seaborn.

Nineteen twenty was also the year the Presbyterian Church burned down. Ern Lundgren was having a shave in Judge Plate's barbershop when the alarm sounded. He ran out half-shaved and half-lathered to go to the rescue. All he was able to save was a basket of trinkets belonging to the Women's Auxiliary, but the women were grateful to him. After the excitement was over, Judge Plate finished Ern's shave.

Reverend John Thompson, recently arrived from Idaho with his wife and daughter, Veola, rebuilt the church in a new location near the foot of the hill behind the town. The new building was generously proportioned, more so than it needed to be for its dwindling body of parishioners. Still, its spaciousness was well suited to the needs of the Port Blakely School, which had no auditorium.

On March 25, 1920, Tamegoro Takayoshi died at age fifty-three. Through all the ups and downs of Port Blakely, he had been a great strength in the Japanese community. His funeral, drawing 150 leaders and friends, was held at the Japanese Baptist Mission.

John Eddy's announcement in 1922 that the mill was to be closed meant that machinery and equipment had to be sold and removed by barge to other locations. In 1924, the company even found a market for the old warehouse, formerly used by the company store, and it was moved by scow from its location on the Port Blakely wharf to Port Orchard. Then the mill itself came down. Pete Murray was in charge of demolition. Some of the timbers and planks in the framework of the mill and the dock were sold, but much of it went into a burn pile—a funeral pyre of what had once been a great, almost living thing. Removal of the wharf decking exposed a beach that was more waterlogged planking and sawdust than rock and gravel. Over the years, when floor timbers in the mill were replaced, the former timbers were often dropped into the water below. There, caught in the piling, they became waterlogged, sank, and literally planked the beach. The forge shops and machine shops were located in several places over the course of those years. Below where they had been, when the deck planking was removed, were found

Remains of the log pond gate at Port Blakely. Photo by Mary Randlett.

sculptures of metal from filings and metal scraps, melted by past fires into shapes that on first sight appear to be enormous conglomerate rock outcroppings.

The log pond no longer served a useful purpose, so the flood gates were removed. Today, the stone masonry work, that formed the walls on which the gates were hung, remains a respectable memorial to the skill of masons long gone.

Before driftwood strewn shores became but a memory, families gathered their wood supply from logs washed from the beach during extreme tides or winter storms. The Nygaards, the Alloins, the Thompsons and other families who lived close to the beach heated their homes from this source. Most of the homes had a rowboat pulled up near them and when the supply of split firewood reached a critical level, family wood-gatherers would stand beside their boat and scan the waves for a good log. When they spotted one, they dragged the boat to water and rowed out to make the capture and tow the log to the beach. Like so much in nature, the supply and demand seemed usually to be in balance. With the help of a peavey, the beached logs were maneuvered up onto blocks to a convenient cutting height. Then the real work began, and each family crosscut its stove and fireplace length blocks from the logs. The wheel-shaped blocks couldn't be wheelbarrowed up to the house, the way the Iturri's had rolled theirs, so they were split on the beach and the winter supply carried up to the woodsheds. Many hours were consumed in the sawing process before a practical steam-driven crosscut saw was developed. That machine was a marvel, and several soon showed up along the shore of the harbor.

The Nygaards from Norway and the Alloins from France arrived on Blakely Harbor just about the time the sawmill's fate was decided. The community, even at that late date, continued to attract foreigners. Quite a few of the new arrivals were fisherman. Like the early immigrants, they had trouble with the language, and it was about this time that the phrase, "Oh, he only speaks halibut English" came into use.

Tamao Takayoshi and her children stayed on until 1925 and, with the Shigemuras, were among the last to leave Yama. Deserted, Port Blakely's best-known suburb was considered a fire hazard and so was torn down.

The ferry <u>Bainbridge</u> arriving at Port Blakely. It served that port and the Country Club for nearly 13 years until September 19, 1937. Its final trip brought to a close 55 years of scheduled boat service to Port Blakely. Photo courtesy Bainbridge Island Historical Society.

Curiously, the year the mill was being dismantled, 1924, was the same year that a ferry slip was built at Port Blakely for the start of auto ferry service from Seattle to the island. Steamers of the Mosquito Fleet touched the island at many points, and one would have thought the island's only auto ferry would have landed at a more central location.

However, some special interests were at work. Most of the people who had the power to influence the location of the ferry terminal lived at the south end of the Island, so that's where the ferry came. The *Liberty*, converted from passenger steamer to auto ferry, was the first vessel on the run and was succeeded in about a year by the handsome new ferry *Kitsap* and a year later by the larger *Bainbridge*. The *Bainbridge* normally made nine trips a day from Seattle into the harbor. From early morning to late at night, its frequent trips gave a nostalgic sense of vitality to the harbor.

In 1924, enrollment at the schoolhouse, remembered by more than forty years of students, still numbered sixty-two. A fall reception was held in the new Presbyterian Church for the teachers in Blakely, Eagledale and West Blakely schools. Port Blakely was still the center of the community; Eagledale, West

Blakely and Pleasant Beach were still the suburbs. But in 1927, the school closed and its pupils transferred to a new school building at Pleasant Beach. There were eight students in the last graduating class.

On August 12, 1928, a hot summer day, the now dilapidated Bainbridge Hotel burned. Its upstairs rooms had been boarded up for some time, and Tailor John Williams had moved from his shop on the street level two or three years earlier. Only the grocery store was still operating in the east wing's lower level. The hotel's once peaked roof was now flat, and the building was an ungraceful eyesore. A fire was about the best thing that could have happened to it. The fireboat *Alki* came over from Seattle and arrived while much of the building was still standing. Since the building no longer had any value, the *Alki's* purpose was to keep the fire from spreading to adjacent houses and the ferry dock. After the embers cooled, Pete Murray had the place cleaned up and one more reminder of what had been was gone.

But now the store was without quarters. The late 1920s were prosperous times before the great crash of the economy in 1929, and Mr. Eddy, having completed demolition of the old sawmill, planned to market home-building sites around the harbor. One of the most obvious needs of such a community was a grocery. It's said that the store site chosen made use of the concrete slab that was once the floor of the big waste burner. A handsome, well-proportioned brick building was designed by Seattle architect Carl F. Gould, using bricks from the long abandoned waste wood burner. The store was to occupy the center part of the building, with the post office in one wing and a small clothing store in the other. The building was built, and with its peaked roof and whitewashed bricks it was a most charming beginning for the new community.

The only problem was that the Great Depression arrived before the full plan could be implemented. Almost no one took to the idea of buying lots and building new homes, the concept the mill company had when it built the store. Instead, as buyers could be found, the mill company sold the old company houses, one by one, and had them removed from their original sites. Some were towed out of the harbor on barges, and others were hauled away by house movers to new locations on the Island.

The Parakeet Tavern took the place of the clothing store. Jack Seaborn's store and the post office opened as scheduled.

In spite of economic conditions, a few mill company lots were sold during the Depression years before the company decided to take them off the market and wait for a better day. Ern Lundgren, of the barbershop and church fire episode, and his wife, Veola Thompson, the minister's daughter, were among the few who bought lots. Theirs was near what had been the center of the community. That was convenient for Ern, who worked on the ferries, and for Veola who cashiered in Jack Seaborn's store.

With the permission of the departed mill company, Ern and Veola built their home from the bricks in the foundation of the mill company office vault. The office had been on the wharf and the vault was so heavy that a tower of bricks had to be built to the beach below to support it. For several years after Pete Murray's crew tore the wharf down, the brick tower remained as an unintended monument to better days. Ern and Veola took down the tower, carried the bricks up the beach, cleaned them and built their house. They finished the house in 1934, and for years it was the only home on Blakely Harbor that measured up in appearance to those in the mill company's ambitious plan.

For Ern, and for his neighbor Gordon Durrell, who also worked on the ferry and who lived in one of the mill company's 1880 frame houses down toward the creek near the former shipyard, the choice of Port Blakely for the island ferry landing was great good fortune. Unfortunately, though, the voice of the population at the south end of the island no longer carried as much weight in Olympia as it once did. So in 1937, the ferry terminal was moved to Eagle Harbor, and, thus, ended fifty five years of scheduled boat service between Port Blakely and Seattle. The *Bainbridge* made her last departure from Port Blakely at 6:30 in the evening on September 19, 1937.

Only one very visible and sometimes still useful tie with 19th century Port Blakely remained, the Masonic Hall. Built under Captain Renton's direction in 1878, it still stood. And it stood until destroyed by fire, the town's nemesis, on the night of November 14, 1955.

Today Blakely Harbor is a favorite anchorage for yacht and

power boat captains, but there is little to remind them of the great mill, the almost living thing, and the vibrant community that surrounded it. On quiet evenings the captains and their friends may talk of those days, but they will listen in vain for the ghostly whine of saws, and search in vain for the tall ships that used to come and go.

All that they will see are some closely cropped pilings in the sand out by the site of the shipyard, some others that mark the site of Captain Renton's original mill and its two successors, and some on the south shore that with imagination can be made into the piling of the railroad barge slip, but really aren't. They will still see the long-abandoned cement building that housed the third mills electrical machinery, and they will still see the now always open entrance to the old log pond. Oh, and if they look carefully, they will see the sculptured pile of filings from the machine shop.

Down near the site of the shipyard, part of its once tall smokestack is now used as a side yard culvert. They won't see that, but if they pick along in the weeds up on the hill, being careful of the poison oak, they might find a chip of church dinner pottery, a piece of washroom mirror from the school or the sole of a discarded logging boot. That's all.

No, there's one thing more they can see if they're willing to walk up the Port Madison Road hill. That's the cemetery. It's deep in the woods just off the old abandoned Port Madison Road. That road hasn't been used for years, so today the entrance is reached from Old Mill Road.

The cemetery, donated by the mill company years ago and conscientiously watched over by community members more than 100 years, is still there. Appropriately enough, it is surrounded still by tall Douglas fir trees on mill company land. Each monument in it seems to speak out, to hold a story. There are monuments to farmer Nils and Fausta Elofson and several of their children; to Nils' brother and his wife, shoemaker Elof and Ane Elofson; to Dr. Cecil Kellam; to Captain August and Charlotte Mattson, his wife, and their daughter, Amanda; to dairy farmer John and Johanna Peterson; to tailor John and Mary Anne Williams; and to the Knights of Pythias who were lost on the *Dix*; to Tomegoro and Tamao Takayoshi; and to Tomegoro's brother, Seinosuke, and his wife, Raku; to Ekoff and Charlotte Nygaard; and to Pete Murray, and Ern and Veola Lundgren. More than 1,100 people have been buried there over the past 100 years. Monuments mark the graves of over 800. Wooden crosses, mostly long gone, must have marked the graves of many others—and still mark some.

Thanks to them all, and to Charles S. Holmes, the Campbells, the Hall Brothers, Sol Simpson of the Blakely Line, George E. Billings, George Monk, Judge Plate, Gus Sanders, Ludvig Oien, Jessie Kellam, John Eddy, D.E. Skinner, Victor Hugo Elfendahl—and to all the others to whom I have introduced you, but especially to Captain William Renton and his wife, Sarah, without whom there might have been no story. They all left a rich history for us.

Post Script

It is now 2005. When the first printing of this book was published in 1989, the Port Blakely Mill Company still owned about 1,100 acres on or adjacent to Blakely Harbor. The company owns almost none today. Developer Kelly Sampson acquired property that was the site of the Eastern Planing Mill and the once-extensive lumber drying and storage yards on the south side of the harbor. Several fine homes have beeen built there. The Bainbridge Island Parks Department dedicated 40-acre Blakely Harbor Park on April 29, 2000. Islandwood, the ambitious dream of Debbi and Paul Brainerd, now owns 250 or more acres on the hill northwest of the mill and surrounding the old Port Blakely Cemetary. Islandwood was created to give children, especially Seattle public school children, an outdoor woodland experience, dedicated to understanding and preserving our environment. The dream has become a nationally-recognized regional asset. Thanks to Blakely Harbor Park and Islandwood and all those working to preserve "open space" on Bainbridge Island, the hills around Blakely Harbor again resemble what they looked like when Captain Renton arrived on the Harbor in 1863—over 140 years ago.

BIBLIOGRAPHY

BOOKS

Bancroft, Hubert H.: Chronicles of the Builders of the Commonwealth, Volume IV, San Francisco, 1892.

Bagley, Clarence: History of King County, Volume I, 1929.

Bagley, Clarence B.: History of Seattle, 1916.

Bass, Sophie Frye: When Seattle Was a Village. 1947. Lowman & Hanford. Seattle, WA.

Beach, Allen W.: Bainbridge Landings. 1960. Driftwood Press. Bainbridge Island, WA.

Birkeland, Captain Torger: Echoes of Puget Sound—Fifty Years of Logging and Steamboating. 1961. The Caxton Printers, Caldwell, ID.

Cameron, James M.: Ships and Seamen of New Glasgow, Nova Scotia.

Coman, Jr., Edwin T. with Gibbs, Helen M.: Time, Tide and Timber—A Century of Pope & Talbot. 1968. Greenwood Press. New York, NY

Ficken, Robert E.: Lumber and Politics—The Career of Mark E. Reed. 1979. The University of Washington Press. Seattle, WA.

Ficken, Robert E.: The Forested Land—A History of Lumbering in Western Washington. 1987. The University of Washington Press. Seattle Grant, Frederic James, Editor: History of Seattle. 1891.

Greenhill, Basil: The Ship—The Life and Death of the Merchant Sailing Ship, 1865–1965. 1980. National Maritime Museum. Greenwich, England.

Hanford, C.H.; Editor of Seattle and Environs, 1852–1924. Pioneer Historical Publishing Company.

Hittell, John S.: Commerce and Industries of the Pacific Coast of North America. 1882. A.L. Bancroft and Co., San Francisco, CA.

Ito, Kazuo: Issei-A History of Japanese Immigrants in North America. 1973. Published in Japan in Japanese and translated by Shinichiro Nakamura and Jean S. Gerard.

Lewis and Dryden: Marine History of the Pacific Northwest. Edited by E. W. Wright. 1961. Antiquarian Press, New York, N.Y.

Marriott, Elsie Frankland: Bainbridge Through Bifocals. 1941. Gateway Printing Company. Seattle, WA.

Masefield, John: The Wanderer of Liverpool. 1930. The MacMillan Company, New York.

McCurdy, H. W.: Marine History of the Pacific Northwest. Edited by George Newell. 1977. Superior Publishing Company, Seattle, WA.

Meeker, Ezra: Pioneer Reminiscences of Puget Sound. 1905. Lowman & Hanford. Seattle, WA

Muir, John: Editor of Picturesque California and the Regions West of the Rocky Mountains from Alaska to Mexico. 1888.

Munro-Fraser, J. P.: History of Santa Clara County, CA. 1881. Alley Bowen & Co., San Francisco, CA.

Parfitt, Elnora and Perry, Freddi and Others, Editors: Kitsap County History—A Story of Kitsap County and Its Pioneers. 1977. Kitsap County Historical Society. Silverdale, WA.

Pelly, Thomas M.: The Story of Restoration Point and The Country Club. 1931. Lowman & Hanford. Seattle, WA.

Perry, Fredi: Port Madison, Washington Territory, 1854–1889. 1989. Perry
    Publishing. Bremerton, WA.
Reed, William G. with Maunder, Elwood R.: Four Generations of
    Management -The Simpson-Reed Story. 1977. Forest History
Society. Santa Cruz, CA.
Roberts, Brian: Editor of They Cast a Long Shadow, A History of the
    Nonwhite Races of Bainbridge Island. 1975. Minority History
Committee of Bainbridge Island School District No. 303
Warner, Katy: A History of Bainbridge Island. 1968. Fourth printing 1978.
Watt, Roberta Frye: The Story of Seattle. 1932. Lowman and Hanford. Seattle.
Weinstein, Robert A.: Tall Ships on Puget Sound—The Marine Photographs
    of Wilhelm Hester. 1978. The University of Washington Press.
    Seattle, WA.
Whittemore, Jeannette C: Skinner and Allied Families. 1937. The American
    Historical Society, New York.

SPEECHES AND UNPUBLISHED MANUSCRIPTS

Hirakawa, Kihachi; Manuscript autobiography.
Howard, Captain Edward: Seventy Years at Sea—Some Incidents in the Life
    of Edward Howard. From a speech given by him in San Francisco
    in 1909 and edited by Captain George Naunton .
Price, Jr., Andrew: Unpublished stories, based on interviews about the
    following families which lived in Port Blakely during the years
    indicated. On deposit at Bainbridge Island Historical Society
    Museum and at Bainbridge Island Public Library, Winslow.
        Elof and Ane Kirstine Elofson, 1890–1916
        Nils and Fausta S. Elofson, 1874–1907
        Hanjiro and Fuji Kono, 1891–1905
        George Richard Emmet Monk and Ann Saunders Monk
        1880–1900
        Torazo and Kuma Hara Nakao, 1901–1962
        Ludvig A. and Freda J. Oien, 1891–1904
        Jons Petter and Johanna Petterson, 1883–1919
        Charles A. and Josephine Plate, 1881–1924
        Eric August and Sarah Ellen Sanders, 1875–1904
        Seinosuke and Raku Takayoshi, 1900–1942
        Tamegoro and Tamao Takayoshi, 1898–1925
        John and Mary Anne McLean Williams, 1900–1933

MAGAZINE ARTICLES AND JOURNALS

Alta California, a magazine: Puget Sound Mills and Shipbuilding. December
    18, 1882. San Francisco.
Berner, Richard C.: The Port Blakely Mill Company, 1876-89. Published in
    the Pacific Northwest Quarterly, Issue #57, October, 1966. Seattle.
Ficken, Robert E. and Sherrard, William R.: The Port Blakely Mill Company,
    1888–1903. Published in Journal of Forest History, Volume 21,
    Number 4, October 1977. Santa Cruz, CA.
McDonald, EvelynWard: The History of Port Blakely.
    "Pacific Lumber and Trade Journal", Seattle, May, 1899.
    "Railway and Marine News", December 15, 1909 on schooner *C. S.
    Holmes*, December, 1916 on Port Blakely schooner Ontario.

Seymore, Captain W. B.: Port Orchard 50 Years Ago, Washington Historical
    Quarterly of the State Historical Society, Volume VIII, 1917.
West Shore Magazine, October, 1882.

UNPUBLISHED LETTERS

Campbell, William, one letter from Boston to John Campbell, written
    October 11, 1849.
Holmes, C. S., one letter to his daughter, Nellie, about a trip to Port
    Blakely and Mason County, WA, written October 22, 1899.
Purvis, James, one letter from Pictou, Nova Scotia to Mrs. Adam Renton,
    Pictou, March 2, 1849.
Renton, William, two letters to his mother in Pictou, one from New Orleans
    dated March 10, 1838 and one from South Shields, Yorkshire,
    England, dated February 21, 1841.
Renton, William and Sarah, twelve letters to his mother in Pictou, nine
    written from Philadelphia between August 18, 1840 and
    June 26, 1849. Two letters from New York dated February 18, 1847,
    and July 24, 1849, and one written Bangor, Maine, dated
    August 11, 1849.
Renton, William Renton, seven letters to his mother in Pictou from Port
    Blakely, May 12, 1866, to August 12, 1868. Three letters to William
    Campbell, Pictou, Nova Scotia, from Port Blakely, November 16,
    1872, March 3, 1873, and October 25, 1873.

NEWSPAPER ARTICLES

Bainbridge Island Beacon, May 16, 1924; October, 1924;
Bainbridge Islander, August 29, 1935.
Bainbridge Review, June 24, 1948; numerous subsequent articles
Kitsap County Herald, May 30, 1902; October 30, 1902; February 9, 1912;
    May 24, 1912;
Northwestern Real Estate and Building Review, Seattle, WA. May 1891
Pacific Tribune, The Weekly, Olympia, WA. February 27, 1869,
    February 5, 1876
Port Orchard Independent, 1901
Puget Sound Weekly Courier, Olympia, WA. July 14, 1882; December 15,
    1882; February 5, 1884; February 26, 1884;
San Francisco Chronicle, August 5, 1927; June 13, 1947;
San Francisco Examiner, August 5, 1927;
Seattle Evening Times, December 21, 1895; September 15, 1896
Seattle Mail and Herald, June 1, 1901
Seattle Post-Intelligencer, October 13, 1880; July 19, 1891; July 28, 1894;
    April 5, 1899; September 1, 1901 April 8, 1902; January 15, 1903;
    March 17, 1903; April 23, 1907; January 16, 1916;
Seattle Press-Times, November 23, 1891; September 28, 1892;
Seattle Times, July 8, 1916; September 21, 1918;
Washington Standard, Olympia, WA. September 24, 1870; February
    5, 1876; December 22, 1877; August 24, 1878; July 16, 1880;
    September 1, 1880; August 18, 1893; April 6, 1895;

LIBRARIES, MUSEUMS and HISTORY SOCIETIES

Archivo Nacional, Santiago, Chile
Bainbridge Island Historical Society Museum, Winslow, WA.
Bancroft Library, University of California, Berkeley, CA.
Jesse Besser Museum, Alpena, Michigan
Bishop Museum, Honolulu, Hawaii
California Historical Society Library, San Francisco, CA.
Columbia River Maritime Museum, Astoria, Oregon
Dalhousie University Archives, Halifax, Nova Scotia
Emigrant Institute, Vaxjo, Sweden
Forest History Society, Inc., Durham, North Carolina
Hector Centre Trust Archives, Pictou, Nova Scotia
Kitsap County Historical Society Museum, Silverdale, WA.
Mason County Historical Society, Inc., Shelton, WA
Museum of History and Industry, Seattle, WA.
National Archives, Washington, D.C.
National Archives, Regional Branch, Seattle, WA.
Nova Scotia Provincial Archives, Halifax, Nova Scotia
Philadelphia Maritime Museum, Philadelphia, PA.
San Francisco Maritime Museum, San Francisco, CA.
Santa Clara County Historical and Genealogical Society, Santa Clara, CA.
J. Porter Shaw Library, Fort Mason, San Francisco, CA.
Seattle Public Library, Seattle, WA.
Smithsonian Institution, Maritime Section, Washington, D.C.
University of Washington Library, Manuscripts Collection, Port Blakely Mill
     Company Records.
University of Washington Library, Northwest History Collection,
     Newspaper clippings of Gordon P. Jones; Photographs in the
     Collection.

DIRECTORIES

Disturnell's Business Directory and Gazetteer of the West Coast of North
     America, Section on Washington Territory, 1882–1883. San
     Francisco, CA.
Great Register of San Francisco for years 1867 through 1873.
Langley's and successor San Francisco Directories for years 1860 to 1924.
McElroy's Philadelphia Directories for years 1844, 1845, 1846.
Pacific Coast Business Directory, Washington Territory section, 1867.
Polk's Directory, Seattle, 1892 and subsequent years.
Washington State Gazeteer, Seattle, For the years 1901 through 1908. Wash-
ington State Grange, Roster of, 1915 and other years (Manzanita #432,
     Island Center #560, Pleasant Beach #564, and Winslow #478).

CEMETERY RECORDS

Monuments of Haliburton Cemetery, Pictou, Nova Scotia
Monuments and Records of Cypress Lawn Cemetery, San Francisco, CA
Monuments and Records of Lake View Cemetery, Seattle, WA
Monuments and Records of Mountain View Cemetery, Oakland, CA
Monuments and Records of Port Blakely Cemetery, Bainbridge Island

APPENDIX

1864...James W. Kean started the first boat service between Port Blakely and Seattle using the sloop *Alexander*.

1869...The 65 foot steamer *Phantom*, starting in Seattle, made a daily circuit of Bainbridge Island. Stops were made at Port Blakely, Freeport, Port Orchard and Port Madison before she returned to Seattle. Her skipper was Captain John Suffern.

1872–1885...The steamer *Success*, built in 1868 on Whidbey Island, made two round trips a day from Port Blakely to Seattle, most of them under Captain James Nugent. The *Success*, 46 feet long, 10 feet wide, and drawing 5 feet 4 inches, was powered by a 12 horsepower engine.

1880...The *Detroit* served briefly on the run to Seattle, perhaps only as a relief vessel.

1885–1889...The *Michigan* was "a diminutive so-called passenger steamer resembling a tug". She served on the Port Blakely to Seattle run under Captain James Nugent.

1889–1905...The *Sarah M. Renton* made two or more round trips to Seattle each day, as required. She was built in 1889 in Port Blakely by the mill company, not Hall Brothers. 91 feet long, 20 feet wide, and 10 feet deep, this steamer was skippered first by Captain W. H. Hobson and later by Captain W. H. Primrose.

1894–1898...The *Favorite*, a 132 foot "ungainly side-wheel steamer, built in 1868 at Utsalady on Camano Island, and modeled after the *Politofsky*, a former Russian gunboat built at Sitka in Russian Alaska", rendered occasional service on the Port Blakely Seattle run during this period. Her principle job was towing logs for the mill company, but she seems often to have been in Port Blakely when pictures were being taken.

1906...The two year old Tacoma built steamer *Dix* replaced the *Sarah M. Renton* this year. She was sunk in one of Puget Sound's worst maritime disasters on November 18th of this same year.

1906–1922...The mill company bought the steamer *Monticello* to replace the *Dix*. She was "a beautiful ship with carpeted cabins and curtained windows." On some of her trips to and from Seattle she stopped at the new dock at the Country Club on the south side of Blakely Harbor.

1923–1926...Auto ferry service began with the converted steamer *Liberty*. Captain C. T. Wyatt was skipper of this 32 car vessel.

1926–1937...The new diesel ferry *Bainbridge* replaced the *Liberty*, and Captain C.T. Wyatt was her skipper. She was built in Houghton on Lake Washington. The steam powered side-wheeler *West Seattle* served as a relief vessel during this period.

September 19, 1937...This was the last day of boat service between Port Blakely and Seattle. The last voyage was made by the *Bainbridge*, and with it ended 55 years of scheduled boat service between Port Blakely and Seattle.

Most of the information above was taken from Bainbridge Landings, a fine booklet by Allen Beach. It was first published in July 1960 by the Driftwood Press.

INDEX